R S S I A

S RANGE

Mt. Kazbek

KHEVSURETI

Cross Pass

SOUTHERN OSSETIA

PSHAVI

Pasanauri

TUSHETI

RANGE

Georgian Military Highway

Aragri R.

Alazani R.

KAKHETI

G I A

Gori

Kura R.

Mtskheta

Telavi

Velistsikhe

Tbilisi ★

KARTLI

ARMENIA

AZERBAIDZHAN

W9-AEO-161

THE
# GEORGIAN
# FEAST

ALSO BY DARRA GOLDSTEIN

*A Taste of Russia*

# THE GEORGIAN FEAST

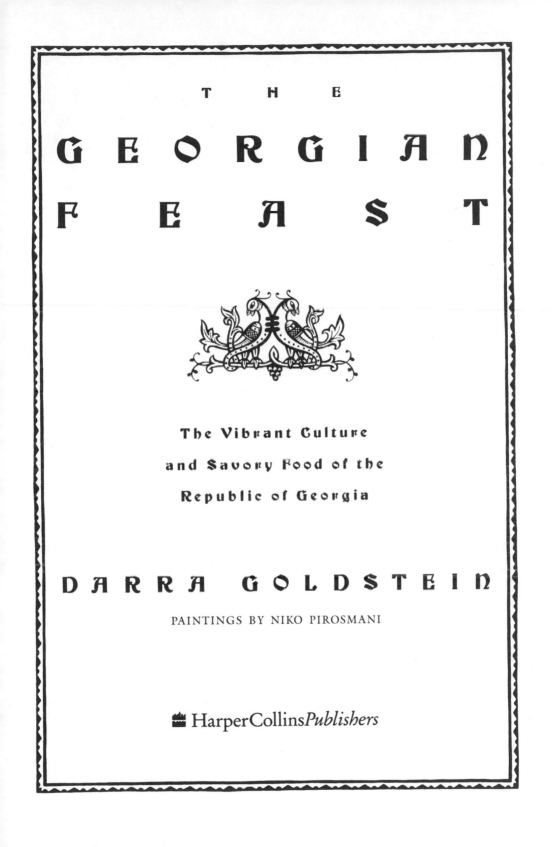

### The Vibrant Culture and Savory Food of the Republic of Georgia

## DARRA GOLDSTEIN

PAINTINGS BY NIKO PIROSMANI

HarperCollins*Publishers*

Grateful acknowledgment is made to the Prints and Photographs Division of the Library of Congress, Washington, D.C., for the use of photographs from its Stereograph Collection (page xxiii), its Prokudin-Gorskii Collection (page 19), and its Harbord Collection (all others); and to Niko Pirosmani for the use of his paintings *Cook* (frontispiece), *Threshing Floor* (page 1), and *Easter Carousal* (detail; page 58).

THE GEORGIAN FEAST: THE VIBRANT CULTURE AND SAVORY FOOD OF THE REPUBLIC OF GEORGIA. Copyright © 1993 by Darra Goldstein. All rights reserved. Printed in the United States of America. No part of this book may be used or reproduced in any manner whatsoever without written permission except in the case of brief quotations embodied in critical articles and reviews. For information address HarperCollins Publishers, Inc., 10 East 53rd Street, New York, NY 10022.

HarperCollins books may be purchased for educational, business, or sales promotional use. For information please write: Special Markets Department, HarperCollins Publishers, Inc., 10 East 53rd Street, New York, NY 10022.

FIRST EDITION

DESIGNED BY JOEL AVIROM
Paintings by Niko Pirosmani
Endpaper map by Paul Pugliese

Library of Congress Cataloging-in-Publication Data

Goldstein, Darra.
The Georgian feast : the vibrant culture and savory food of the Republic of Georgia / Darra Goldstein.—1st ed.
p. cm.
Includes bibliographical references and index.
ISBN 0-06-016646-0
1. Cookery, Georgian (Georgian S.S.R.) 2. Cookery—Georgia (Republic) 3. Food habits—Georgia (Republic) 4. Georgia (Republic)— Description and travel. I. Title.
TX723.4.G65 1992 92-53373
641.5947'95—dc20

93 94 95 96 97 DT/RRD 10 9 8 7 6 5 4 3 2 1

*For my parents, Irving and Helen Haft Goldstein,*
*who taught me the joys of the table*

# CONTENTS

# ACKNOWLEDGMENTS

**M**any people helped in the creation of this book. In Georgia, I am particularly indebted to Zaza and Marina Gachechiladze, who hosted me in Tbilisi and enabled me to travel throughout Georgia to sample regional specialties. Without the help of Alex Rondeli, I would not have met Georgi Gorgodze and Shalva Lobzhanidze of the Georgian Ministry of Trade, who took the time to discuss their vast knowledge of Georgian cuisine and to answer my endless queries; or Georgi Dzhomardzhidze and Nugzar Bagaturia at Tbilisi's Food Industry Research Institute, who gave me a wealth of information about the nutritional and chemical composition of Georgian foods. Nugzar also collected scarce cookbooks to send me. Luka Nikashvili and his host of chefs in Telavi taught me much about the foodways of Kakheti. Ira Kandelaki and Mzia Gachechiladze shared with me their kitchen expertise. And Misha Kalinichev took the trouble to provide me with the Latin names for many plants and spices used in Georgian cooking.

My wonderful and enterprising agent, Susan Lescher, showed immediate enthusiasm for the project. And without the expert guidance and saintly patience of my editor, Susan Friedland, this book would not have taken its present shape. I am also very grateful to Jack Shoemaker, who supported the book in its early stages; and to Frank Kane, who introduced me into the world of Georgianists and translated an important glossary for me. I can't imagine a better researcher than Steven Fagin, whose knowledge of Georgian, reliability, and indefatigable efforts proved invaluable. Both Alice Arndt and Dodona Kiziria helped with specific queries, while Joyce Toomre and Ilona Bell offered valuable advice on the entire manuscript. Henry Art provided helpful answers to my botanical queries. Williams College gave timely and generous assistance reproducing photographs. My parents, Irving and Helen Haft Goldstein, labored cheerfully in the kitchen, testing recipes. Finally, my husband, Dean Crawford, deserves great thanks for his unflagging support and keen editing, as well as for those extra hours of childcare.

*Georgian men in traditional costume posing for a feast.*

# INTRODUCTION

**R**emote as Georgia may seem, this small nation once occupied a pivotal place in the world. Georgia was much featured in the mythology of ancient times, chronicled by historians and travelers who ventured to the farthest reaches of the known classical world. Stretching from the Black Sea to the Caspian, Georgia lay athwart important East-West trade routes. Through the vagaries of history, Georgia enjoyed independence one thousand years ago, only to be subsumed by the Russian Empire in the nineteenth century. More recently, the republic existed within the borders of the Soviet Union. In 1991, the Soviets' relaxed hold on their constituent republics allowed the proud and restive Georgians to proclaim independence. With a number of contending political groups, Georgia today finds itself in flux. Yet it still represents a Shangri-la of bounty, tucked away in mountain valleys and fertile lowlands.

The Russians are only the latest in a series of foreign powers to have dominated Georgia, and a state of agitation is hardly new to this country, which has endured centuries of turmoil. Remarkably, however, through all the invasions, sieges, and subjugations, Georgia has managed to maintain a strong national identity. This societal pride is something greater than patriotism, more akin to a religious belief in the sacredness of the earth and its ability to sustain. Gathered around the feast table, Georgians like to retell the tales of how their land was made. One of their favorite creation myths finds the first Georgians seated under a pergola at a table laden with wine and food. So engrossed are they in feasting on grilled lamb with plum sauce and garlicky roasted eggplant that they miss God's deadline for choosing a country, and the world is divided up without them. His task complete, God sets off for home, only to find the Georgians still merrily toasting and singing. God stops to reproach them for their negligence, but the *tamada*, the toastmaster, is not worried that the Georgians have no place to live. They have spent their time well, he explains, thanking

God in lavish toasts for having created such a magnificent world. Pleased that the Georgians have not forgotten Him, God rewards them with the very last spot on earth, the one He had been saving for Himself. And so it was that the Georgians came to live in paradise.

Another myth is slightly less reverent. While creating the world, God wisely took a break for supper. But He became so involved in His meal that He inadvertently tripped over the high peaks of the Caucasus range, spilling a little of everything from His plate onto the land below. So it was that Georgia came to be blessed with such riches, table scraps from Heaven.

Georgia's topography is indeed varied. The country embraces both alpine and subtropical zones in an area smaller than Scotland or South Carolina. Nearly four-fifths of Georgia is mountainous, making the various regions quite self-contained, each with its own customs and culinary traditions. The Likhi Range, running north to south, effectively divides the country in half. Western Georgia, bordering on the Black Sea, is marked by high precipitation and steamy temperatures. Here tea and citrus fruits thrive. Eastward the climate grows progressively drier; sere Central Asian winds buffet the plateaus east of the Likhi chain. This hot, dry atmosphere produces the lush fruits and grapes of the Kartli and Kakheti provinces.

The area around the Black Sea, the Euxine of the Ancients, boasts the older civilization. The Georgians trace their own culture back to the sixth century B.C., but other peoples inhabited this region beginning around the fifteenth century B.C. From the outset the populace profited from the native riches of the coastal region, which the Greeks knew as Colchis. Here the wealthy King Aeetes had his dynasty. Homer refers to Aeetes and his legendary land in the *Odyssey,* when he tells of Jason's exploits. It was to Colchis that Jason and his Argonauts sailed in search of the Golden Fleece. Most likely a golden fleece did exist—a sheepskin used to trap nuggets of gold from the mountain streams. More momentous for Jason than the Fleece, however, was his discovery of Medea, King Aeetes's daughter. Medea was renowned for her herbal sorcery. No matter that she used one of her potent concoctions to poison their children when Jason abandoned her, Georgian folk etymology still connects the word *medicine* with Medea's name, since before resorting to vengeance she was the first healer, the first to use plants for their curative powers, a practice that still prevails in Georgia today.

Impressed by the progressive agriculture of the early Georgians, the Greeks established the colonies of Bathys (Batumi), Phasis (Poti), Pitiunt (Pitsunda), and Dioscurias (Sukhumi) along the Black Sea coast. But Greek control came to an end in 66 B.C. when Pompey invaded, and the area fell under Roman authority. As documented by such classical historians and geographers as Herodotus, Strabo, Pliny, and Ptolemy, Greeks and Romans alike considered outposts in Colchis important links in the trade route to Persia. From the Black Sea ships could sail up the Phasis River (today's Rioni), then travel by portage over the Likhi Range to the Kura River Valley, continuing overland to Persia.

From the earliest times Georgia's central geography and fabled riches beckoned outsiders. As the centuries passed, merchants established caravansaries throughout the country, and by the early middle ages the capital city of Tbilisi had become a major stopover on the medieval trade routes, a midpoint between Moslem East and Christian West. Travelers left journals describing the wild landscapes and exotic customs they encountered.

Both Marco Polo and Friar William of Rubruck mention Georgia in their travel notes, and Sir John Chardin, on a seventeenth-century visit, extravagantly praised the abundance of the land:

> Georgia is as fertile a country as any can be imagin'd, where a man may live both deliciously and very cheap. Their Bread is as good as any in the World; their Fruit is delicious and of all sorts. Neither is there any part of Europe that produces fairer Pears and Apples, or better tasted, nor does any part of Asia bring forth more delicious Pomegranates. Cattel is very plentiful and very good, as well the larger sort as the lesser. Their Fowl of all sorts is incomparable, especially their Wild-Fowl; their Boars-Flesh is as plentiful and as good as any in Colchis. . . . The Caspian Sea which is next to Georgia and the Kurr, that runs through it, supplies it with all sorts of salt and fresh Fish, so that we may truly say that there is no country where a Man may have an Opportunity to fare better than in this.
>
> —*The Travels of Sir John Chardin into*
> *Persia and the East-Indies . . .* (1686)

Travelers kept mainly to the established trade routes, rarely venturing into the highlands that loom north of the fertile plains. Chardin did not experience the romance of these intimidating, inspiring mountains, which give shape and definition to the Georgian land. The Caucasus have also given birth to many a legend. The earliest tales tell of fierce women warriors inhabiting the mountains. These were the Amazons, a matriarchal society whose adherents did not flinch at cutting off a breast in order to use their bows more effectively. Then came Prometheus, who stole the secret of fire from the gods and in punishment was chained to Mount Kazbek, destined for eternal torment as an eagle pecked at his liver, which continually regenerated itself. Further west on Mount Elbrus, Noah's dove is said to have alighted before flying on to the ark grounded at Ararat. And what of the mysterious Tamara? This Caucasian Lorelei enticed travelers to their deaths as they passed through the Daryal Gorge of the Terek River.

Between the sheer cliffs rising on either side of this gorge, the Terek cuts a raging swath, making for hazardous passage. No less an explorer than Alexander the Great is said to have struggled through these mountain chasms, though in truth only a legendary Alexander, not the historical one, ventured here. Yet popular mythology persists, identifying the Daryal Gorge as the original site of Alexander's Gate, a massive barrier of iron and steel built to keep the northern barbarians, Gog and Magog, from penetrating the pass. Here Alexander supposedly had a rendezvous with Thalestris, Queen of the Amazons. According to the Latin history by Quintus Curtius, Thalestris's passion for Alexander was so great that she demanded he spend thirteen days satisfying her desire before renewing his campaigns. Thalestris hoped to produce a strong female infant for her Amazon tribe; however, she assured Alexander that if a boy were born, he could take the child for his heir. To the disappointment of his readers, Quintus Curtius does not reveal the outcome of their legendary union.

Today the Daryal Gorge is less impressive than in mythological times. How perilous the passage was for early travelers negotiating the steep, rutted path! When camels stumbled, whole caravans tumbled into the misty depths below. Later, carriages frequently broke their axles and clung precipitously to the brink, waiting for help to arrive. Now hydroelectric stations have tamed the mighty Terek, and a modern road has eliminated most of the hair-raising curves and abrupt descents of the wilder, bygone days. Even so, the highway is terrifying enough to traverse in a Soviet auto fueled by low-octane gas, driven by an antic Georgian flirting with the cliff face. The scenery remains spectacular; the precipice, near enough to touch with your hand.

Modern travelers still experience vertigo until the road levels out onto the broad, windblown plateau of the Cross Pass, the highest point on the highway. Here the vista is magnificent. One feels on top of the world, close to the gods, near the very cradle of civilization, yet in a wild, isolated place. Beyond the pass the road descends, meandering through alpine meadows brilliant with snow in winter, glorious with wildflowers in summer. Shepherds' huts cling to the mountainside, the only sign of habitation for miles. Apart from improvements to roads and villages, the landscape has hardly changed since antiquity. Here is how Georgia appeared to the Russian writer Anton Chekhov when he visited there in the late nineteenth century:

> . . . I saw marvellous things. . . . My impressions were so new and sharp that all I experienced seems a dream, and I can't believe it. I saw the sea in all its vastness, the Caucasian shore, mountains, mountains, mountains, eucalyptuses, tea plants, waterfalls, pigs with long pointed snouts, trees wrapped in lianas like veils, clouds spending the night on the breast of giant cliffs, dolphins, fountains of oil, subterranean fires, a fireworshippers' temple, mountains, mountains, mountains. . . . I survived the Georgian Military Highway. It isn't a highway, but poetry, a marvellous, fantastic story. . . . Can you imagine yourself at a height of 8000 feet? . . . Are you imagining it? Now in your mind go to the edge of the abyss and look down; far, far below you see a narrow basin, along which winds a small white ribbon—the white-haired, grumbling Aragvi River . . .
>
> —Anton Chekhov, letter of August 12, 1888,
> to K. S. Barantsevich

Not all who passed through the Caucasus were as pacific as Chardin and Chekhov, content to meditate on Georgia's wonders. Nomad horsemen periodically swept down through the mountains from the northern steppes, routing villages and destroying crops. Even more violent were the frequent incursions by Georgia's mighty neighbors to the east and west, both of whom sought to dominate its resources. Western Georgia, or Colchis, faced the world of classical civilization—first Rome, then Byzantium—while the eastern half, the ancient Iberia, looked to Persia. Georgia's geographical position between the two contending powers of Christendom and Islam brought repeated misfortune to the country as it was buffeted by both sides. The common greeting among Georgians, *gamardzhoba,* is equivalent to our "hello," but its original meaning, "victory," attests to the frequency of battles the people endured. Even though caught in the middle, Georgians managed to preserve their country's own unmistakably Georgian character, an intriguing blend of East and West.

Despite its split orientation, Georgia perceived itself as a separate political entity as early as the fourth century B.C. when King Farnavazi, Georgia's first native ruler, imposed some political order on the country. Farnavazi also introduced the ornate, lapidary script of the Georgian alphabet, an early literacy the Georgians are rightfully proud of. Because their national identity dates back so many centuries, the Georgians have a long historical perspective that allows them to take their overlords less seriously than other peoples who have more recently been overrun. Although the battles against Persians, Turks, Mongols, Bolsheviks, and other aggressors are legendary, for most of their troubled history the Georgians have learned to live in peace with those who invaded them—after an initial period of fierce resistance, of course.

But even the lowest points in Georgia's history could not stifle the innate spirit of the Georgian people, renowned for their joie de vivre. This attitude is encapsulated in a comment once made by the Symbolist poet Grigol Robakidze. Describing the fear and chaos following the Bolshevik occupation of Georgia in 1921, Robakidze noted, "All around, everything was crumbling, and Tbilisi remained the only city that greeted this destruction with a song."

The complex Georgian attitude toward outsiders can be seen in the huge statue of Mother Georgia that towers over present-day Tbilisi. In one hand Mother Georgia holds high a bowl of wine; in the other she carries a sword. The figure herself gazes inscrutably ahead, prepared for either friend or foe, as if heeding the proverb that "an enemy may come as far as the door of your house, but once he enters, he is a friend." The ensuing commensal activity is not taken lightly: The Georgian word for friend, *megobari,* signifies "one who has eaten from the same *gobi,*" or bowl. Georgia's traditional hospitality is rooted in the intricacies of her long relationships with invaders.

Under their latest subjugation, the Georgians continued to celebrate their national identity with seemingly endless feasting and toasting; independence whetted their jubilation. As they toast, Georgians often invoke God's name, though a vital spirituality is far more important to them than religious dogma. The early Georgians, like other pagan peoples, had a highly devout relationship to their surroundings even before accepting Christianity in the fourth century. It is telling that the Georgians' acceptance of the Christian faith was tied up with their deep love for the land and for the good life. Unlike the Moslems around them, Georgians put the fruit of the vine to good—and extensive—use.

*A display of Georgian grapes and wines at a Tiflis exhibition.*

For a Georgian, wine evokes a sense of culture and community. Based on evidence of grape pips unearthed during archeological digs, viticulture is an ancient art in Georgia, practiced as early as the fourth millennium B.C. Scientists believe the species *vitis vinifera,* the original wine grape, to be native to the Caucasus region, while many linguists consider the Georgian word for wine, *ghvino,* the prototype for such Indo-European variations as *vino, vin, wine, Wein.* The earliest vines were grown on land belonging to the pagan temples, and a cult of Dionysus grew up, with the vine the iconic representation of an agrarian deity. Thus the early Georgians not only cultivated the grape, but worshiped it, too. In the yard the *marani,* or wine storage shed, stood like a sacred temple, just as in the home the hearth stood like a symbolic altar.

Georgians depict the archetypal Tree of Life as a plane tree entwined with vines. The vine symbolizes both life and faith, a belief that

Saint Nino of Cappadocia adapted to Christian doctrine when she introduced it to Georgia in the fourth century. Bearing a cross plaited of dried vines and tied with her own hair, Saint Nino seemed to represent divine approval for the winemaking that had been practiced for centuries. The vine and the cross became inextricably entwined, each an object of devotion. In this way the advent of Christianity served to elevate the importance of viticulture, just as the focus on wine helped to lubricate the conversion.

Strange as it may seem, even a century after the Georgian nation had converted to Christianity, the capital city of Tbilisi, founded in the fifth century, remained a Moslem city-state under Persian control. In fact, until 1936 the world knew Tbilisi by its Persian name of Tiflis. This foreign appellation not only attests to the city's long years of subjugation but also masks its romantic beginnings. Legend tells that the fifth-century King Vakhtang Gorgaslani, out on a hunt near the Kura River, killed a pheasant which he retrieved fully cooked from the hot springs where it had fallen. Naturally, a feast ensued. Toasting his good fortune, Gorgaslani vowed to create a city on this auspicious spot, which he called "Tbilis-kalaki" or "Warm City." But Tbilisi's fate proved to be less than auspicious. Between its designation as the capital of Iberia, or eastern Georgia, in the sixth century and its absorption into the Russian Empire in the early nineteenth century, the city was sacked forty times. Following a mid-seventh century Arab invasion, Tbilisi remained under Arab rule for over four hundred years.

Only in the ninth century when the Bagrationi dynasty came into power did Georgia begin to exert itself as a strong Christian nation. The early tenth century saw the rise of an independent feudal monarchy, and during the reign of David the Builder (1089–1125) Tbilisi was finally freed from foreign control. Under the rule of the great queen Tamara (1184–1212), Georgia reached the height of its civilization, experiencing a renaissance a good two hundred years before Italy. Long before the founding of Oxford or Heidelberg, the Gelati Academy in the western province of Imereti had developed into an important school of philosophy, which also practiced advanced teachings in astronomy, medicine, and music. (The main church of Gelati still stands, adorned with beautiful obsidian mosaics and commanding an impressive view of the surrounding hills.) In eastern Georgia, the arts and sciences were assiduously pursued in the famous school at Ikalto. It was here that Shota Rustaveli, the author of Georgia's great

*The twelfth-century Gelati monastery surrounded by cornfields.*

epic poem *The Knight in the Panther's Skin,* is said to have studied. Rustaveli's epic is striking not only for its beautiful language and lilting cadences, but also for the strong heroines it portrays.

Sadly, Georgia's Renaissance was cut short by a new threat from outside: the Golden Horde. In 1225 invading Mongols from Central Asia destroyed Tiflis. However, after their rampages the Mongols, unlike the Persians, allowed the Georgian Orthodox Church to flourish and daily life to proceed, as long as the necessary tributes were forthcoming. So despite an end to its period of great flowering, Georgia was able nevertheless to remain relatively prosperous and stable throughout its Mongol occupation, which lasted until the early fourteenth century.

New troubles arrived when Tamerlane's armies attacked in 1386. Unlike his precursors, Tamerlane was wanton and ruthless, killing and devastating wherever he went. He even penetrated beyond the Likhi Range into western Georgia, an area the Mongols had spared. Because it lacked a strong leader, Georgia's recovery from Tamerlane's aggression was slow. For the next several centuries the country once again fell prey to campaigns by the Persians as well as by the newly strong Ottoman Turks, who had gained ascendance after Constantinople fell in 1453. Although politics and allegiances kept shifting in the countries that bordered Georgia, the Georgians ineluctably found themselves trapped in the middle. Only Armenia to the south, a second island of Christianity in the Islamic world, presented no threat.

By the late sixteenth century Georgia was effectively split in two, with western Georgia falling under the Turkish sphere of influence, and eastern Georgia politically part of northwest Iran. But the region's balance of power began to change as Russia came into its own, testing its new imperial might in Siberia and the Caucasus, where it built Cossack outposts in the northern highlands. Exhausted from the continual parrying between Persians and Turks, the Georgians expressed interest in their Christian neighbors to the north. But their flirtation with Russia served only to anger Persia, which initiated a new series of violent campaigns against them.

Repeated attacks from the Persians, the Turks, and Moslem tribesmen in Daghestan to the north finally caused the Georgians to turn actively to Russia for help. In 1783 King Irakli II, the beleaguered successor to the ancient Bagrationi dynasty, signed the Treaty of Georgievsk, acknowledging Russia's sovereignty. His signing was a sad day in the history of the Georgian nation. Today many Russians look down on Georgians as half-civilized and unpredictable, but the fact is that Russia's acceptance of Christianity in 988 followed the Georgians' by many centuries, as did its receipt of an alphabet. Thus King Irakli's capitulation represented to the Georgians a terrible concession to a less ancient, and to their minds less cultured, society.

Despite the promise of his name, the Georgian form of Hercules, Irakli did not have much choice. As a weak Christian nation besieged on three sides by the Moslem world, Georgia logically turned to the powerful protector to the north. But instead of allowing the Georgians to maintain control over their internal affairs as the Treaty of Georgievsk had stipulated, Russia incorporated Georgia into its empire in 1801 in an attempt to protect itself against the ever more menacing Turks. Army garrisons were set up in remote mountain regions, making the Russian military presence in the Caucasus increasingly strong. Workers began the arduous task of constructing the Georgian Military Highway, a road that would eventually connect Tbilisi with the new Russian city of Vladikavkaz, "Ruler of the Caucasus." (The Russians never hesitated to proclaim their imperial pretensions.) The Georgian Military Highway followed the ancient and perilous route through the mountains, passing through the Daryal Gorge. Up until the second half of the nineteenth century, Moslem tribes led by the valiant Shamyl were engaged in an early form of guerrilla warfare. The Russians attempted to help travelers by establishing a few dismal posts along the highway where an escort through the most difficult reaches could be arranged, but the ferocious mountaineers, waging a thirty-year struggle against Russian rule, often abducted the strangers crossing their territory. The Russians finally captured Shamyl in 1859, but his legend lives on, contributing to the rich lore of the Caucasus.

No less an adventurer than Alexandre Dumas visited the Caucasus during Shamyl's reign. His travel memoirs tell of negotiating the narrow passes of the highway under heavy guard, in constant danger of attack by the roving mountaineers. "Nowhere else," he wrote, "even in Algeria, even in the Atlas Mountains, have I found travelling so exhausting, so fraught with danger, as in the Caucasus." But Dumas père reveled in risk and adventure. One evening at dusk his group had to pass through a particularly dangerous defile, and everyone was wary. Suddenly, a covey of partridge, disturbed by the noise of the entourage, flew up from the bushes. Dumas could not restrain himself. He leapt out of his carriage to shoot a plump bird for supper.

Once the Russian army garrisons were established, Georgia became a favored place of exile for political prisoners, its remoteness earning it the nickname "the Siberia of the South." The soldiers, reluc-

*A typical homestead in Svaneti.*

tant at first to be sent to such a distant post, discovered that Georgia was indeed beautiful and exotic, and the Russian people soon grew fascinated with this mountainous, romantic land. The poet Mikhail Lermontov acknowledged the power Georgia held over its northern visitors, stating that "if you go to the Caucasus, you'll return a poet." Even such deeply Russian writers as Tolstoy and Chekhov were moved to visit Georgia. Following a trip there in 1852 Tolstoy commented that "I find that a great moral change has taken place in me . . . here I have become a better man." And Chekhov wrote that in Georgia "nature astonishes one to the point of madness and despair."

The Russian presence in Georgia continued unabated until 1918 when, following the October Revolution, Georgia declared its independence. The country's elation was shortlived, however. Although the two countries had signed a noninterference treaty in 1920, for the second time the Russians disregarded their agreement, and Georgia's hopes for reclaiming its ancient glory quickly evaporated. In 1921 Bolshevik troops invaded, and once again Georgia was incorporated into a stronger empire, this time the Soviet Union. As small and prosperous homesteads were amalgamated into massive collective farms, morale sagged. The Georgians could not rally enthusiasm to work for the great communal enterprise. Many did, however, become successful profiteers, transporting scarce fruits to northern cities during the winter months to sell to the citrus starved Russians at extremely high prices. Anyone who has traveled by Aeroflot between Tbilisi and Moscow may anxiously recall seats and aisles piled high with sacks full of produce in complete disregard for safety.

Unlike White Russians and neighboring Armenians who fled the newly created Soviet state in vast numbers, most Georgians chose to remain behind despite the difficult circumstances. Their ties to the land were simply too strong. The few who did leave established Georgian organizations abroad to help preserve their culture, and notably, even in emigration their devotion to their native food did not die. Throughout the world Georgians found that they could operate successful restaurants, even in the most remote places. More than one White Russian exile has written of the excellent railway buffets run by Georgians in Manchuria.

During the period of Soviet rule most of the outside world knew Georgia only as the birthplace of Joseph Stalin. The issue of Stalin is a sticky one for Georgians. Born Iosif Dzhugashvili, Stalin is unquestionably Georgia's most famous native son, and as such he is still revered by many—an embarrassment to those Georgians who do not place national pride before all else. Visitors are often alarmed to see a photograph of a smiling Stalin dangling from the mirror of a taxicab manned by a seemingly friendly driver. But this homage has nothing to do with the evils Stalin perpetrated; rather it reflects a misguided national spirit. Georgians are self-conscious about being so little known and rightly afraid of being overlooked. Stalin, at least, brought Georgia to the attention of the world. And although he was an evil force, it cannot be denied that he was a towering figure of the twentieth century. His name is known; his importance to history cannot be dismissed. Hence the ambivalence with which many regard him in Georgia. Educated Georgians find this reverence especially difficult to understand, considering the special cruelty that Stalin meted out to his own people, a point made very clear in Tenghiz Abuladze's 1988 film, *Repentance*. Not only were thousands of Georgians banished from their villages to the Siberian wastelands, but ethnic Georgians were more than proportionally represented in the labor camps, even though their republic, on the outskirts of the Soviet Union, represented no threat to the political center. Both Stalin and his henchman (and fellow countryman) Lavrenty Beria used the occasion of the purges to settle old scores and retaliate against those who had shunned or slighted them when they were first rising to power in Georgia.

Stalin's figure continues to loom large today as his misdeeds are publicly recounted, causing old resentments to flare up between Russians and Georgians. And recent ethnic strife within Georgia has compounded tensions. When the Soviet government carved up the Caucasus, it created two separate political entities within the borders of the Georgian Republic—South Ossetia, in the southern Caucasus, and Abkhazia, on the Black Sea. Encouraged by Georgia's successful independence movement, the Ossetians and Abkhazians are now seeking autonomy. Georgia again finds itself in turmoil caused by shifting political balances.

However precarious the national situation, the Georgians cling fiercely to their land and traditions. Their loyalty can be fervid, expressed during toasts and meals as an act of consecration. In acknowledging their land as a gift from heaven, the Georgians express their most deeply felt values. And by preparing sumptuous feasts, they exalt the fruits of the earth.

PART I

# AN ABUNDANT LAND

*A proud Svan with dagger and waterproof cape.*

# I

# A Cultural Excursion

ost visitors to Georgia arrive by plane from Moscow, disembarking at the faintly colonial airport in Tbilisi. Much more appealing (and appropriate) is to discover Georgia as the ancients did, arriving from the west on the Black Sea. Now that travel restrictions have been eased, there is a legal point of entry at Sarpi, a somnolent village across the border from the Turkish town of Hopa. Border crossings into the former Soviet Union always had a chill about them, but even by the relaxed standards of 1989, entering Georgia directly, by way of Turkey, was a surprise. As soon as the customs official learned whom my husband and I would be visiting in Tbilisi, he broke into a broad grin—he knew our friend from the university. The extended family that is Georgian society reaches to its most remote outposts, and so we were effusively welcomed to Georgia, the uniformed official transformed magically into a host. He even offered us a ride into town. We declined, however, knowing that dozing under a nearby acacia tree our friend awaited us.

Our friend maneuvered his car unfazed among cows, pigs, and chickens, the true proprietors of Georgian highways. Every so often, we passed appealing roadside stands offering corn on the cob, baskets of ripe feijoas, and fresh hazelnuts still green and chewy in their husks. Unable to resist an immediate taste of Georgia, we pulled up alongside a large eucalyptus under which an old man, his face bronzed and creased from the sun, was tending a makeshift brazier. The old man grinned eagerly, choosing several choice ears of white corn for us,

3

which he dropped into the boiling water. The corn was so tender and sweet that we hardly minded burning our fingers.

This southern section of the coast, called Adzharia, enjoys the highest precipitation in Georgia, and the resulting agricultural riches are very much in evidence. Citrus groves and tea plantations stretch for miles. Adzharia produces Georgia's largest yields of tea and tangerines. Farmers also grow tobacco, plums, apricots, figs, pomegranates, feijoas, olives, medlar, persimmons, and grapes. Particularly prized are the bluish-black Izabella grapes, "fleshy and healthy like a cluster of night itself," as the Russian poet Osip Mandelstam described them. Land is so intensively cultivated here that grape vines are trained to grow up the trunks of the fruit trees to save space, making for picturesque orchards when the ripe grapes dangle invitingly from the tops of the trees beside plums, apricots, or olives. This method of training vines, known as *maglari* in Georgian, has been practiced since ancient times. To harvest the grapes from such heights, special elongated baskets are raised on cords. In some homesteads we saw another decorative practice, called *okekhnari,* which trains the grapes up columns or other vertical structures. A crossbeam placed at the top encourages the vines to grow together in a canopy, offering shade from the sun as well as a lovely arbor for an al fresco meal. Along the roads in fields and yards bristle *nalis*, food storage huts on stilts, often five feet or more above the ground.

In contrast to such intense agricultural activity, the cuisine of this part of Georgia seems almost indolent. Many of the local recipes are borrowed from neighboring Turkey, and even those typically Georgian are marked by unusual simplicity. As in other subtropical areas, it is easy in Adzharia simply to live off the land. When fruits grow lush and ripe for the picking, why not enjoy their pure taste and dispense with complex preparations? More surprising, though, is the apparent indifference of those along Georgia's Black Sea coast to the fruits of the sea. Surely an indigenous cuisine would make use of the bountiful seafood and fish. Just a few miles west, Turks rhapsodize over the sturgeon, turbot, and fresh *hamsi* or anchovies that are regularly pulled from the sea. But Georgian cuisine never developed an exciting repertoire of saltwater fish or seafood dishes; instead, most of its fish recipes utilize the freshwater varieties plentiful in rivers and lakes. Two high-altitude lakes in this area of western Georgia are famous for the fish they breed, Lake Paliastomi near Poti and Lake Ritsa near Pitsunda,

*An elevated corn barn in western Georgia.*

nearly 3,000 feet above sea level. As for the Black Sea, some flatfish are prepared according to local custom by gentle poaching in red wine, with the stock used as the basis for a nut sauce. In the coastal city of Batumi, however, grilled meat is still the order of the day.

One explanation for the relative disregard for fish is that for many years the swampy lowlands of the region and the mosquitoes they bred kept the local population small. Until malaria was finally eradicated in this century, most people preferred to live in the mountains. In their remote settlements they were not entirely free from predation, however, though here the enemy was human rather than insect. When the Turks seized possession of western Georgia in the sixteenth century, they fostered an extensive slave trade. Children were regularly kidnapped and sold as chattel to wealthy families in distant countries. In fact, the influential warrior caste of Mamelukes in Egypt derived from these young slaves. From their lowly status as vassals to caliphs and sultans, the Mamelukes rose to positions of power, eventually coming to rule over their former masters. Circassian chicken, so enjoyed in the Middle East, originated with the slaves from the western Caucasus.

Although Georgians adopted none of Turkey's expertise with fish, other evidence of Turkish influence can be found among the large Islamic population still inhabiting the coastal area. The day we crossed the border into Georgia happened to be a Moslem religious holiday, when everything in Turkey was closed. Religious holidays were not officially celebrated in Georgia (or any other part of the then Soviet Union), but the family we stayed with near Batumi offered us a ritual sweet similar in taste to Turkey's famous *helva* or semolina pudding, only firmer in texture. Another specialty we enjoyed in Adzharia is *achma-makarina*, noodle dough layered with cheese like the *makarna firinda* we sampled in Istanbul. One of the most frequently encountered foods in this region is the stuffed vegetable or *dolma*, known in Georgian as *tolma*. Surprisingly, though, the tradition of *mezze* or appetizers found in most Middle Eastern countries is not part of the food culture here. Rather, the Georgian way of dining prevails, with main and supporting courses offered simultaneously.

Farming in this coastal area is not confined to the valleys but also practiced on the steep hillsides, which are expertly terraced to take advantage of all possible space. Along the roadsides extend acres of bushy plants with glossy leaves. These are the tea plantations. The leaves for the best tea are still picked largely by hand, and the green expanses of fields are dotted with the colorful scarves and blouses of laborers. From time to time the air fills with a cloying, almost narcotic smell, the odor of tea leaves being processed and refined. Tea was not introduced into Georgia until the nineteenth century and became a major cash crop only in the Soviet period. Thus its consumption is a relatively recent phenomenon. The Georgians still prefer Turkish coffee. Throughout the coastal region cafés are less likely to brew tea than to offer demitasse cups of strong coffee with a glass of cold water on the side.

This custom certainly prevails in Batumi, Georgia's largest coastal town. Except for the absence of epidemic, the city has changed little since Osip Mandelstam visited there in 1923:

A greenhouse. A hummingbird city. A city of palm trees in tubs.
A city of malaria and gentle Japanese hills. A city resembling the
European quarter in any colonial country, ringing with mosquitoes in the summer and offering fresh tangerines in December.
—from "Mensheviks in Georgia"

Batumi retains its color even today. At the southern edge of Georgia's coast, it lies less than twenty miles from Turkey. Entering the city, the visitor steps back in time to a more unhurried way of life, where families and lovers still stroll for long hours along the seaside promenade, admiring the bathers and the boats moored offshore. Batumi is neither sleek nor rich, but lush from the exotic flora and fauna that thrive in its subtropical air. It is a resort town, down-at-the-heels. The air is heavy with languor, and things move more slowly here than in the rest of Georgia. Even the traffic lingers, or lumbers along the steep, winding roads leading into the hills above the city.

Batumi feels like a colonial city, with a shared past. Its buildings do not look distinctively Georgian, resembling instead the architecture in other colonized parts of the world, with airy white buildings, paddle fans, verandas, and the promise of leisure. Foghorns and buoy bells in the channels add to the allure of this port city, but the shipping and petroleum industries have taken their toll—in many places the shore is marred by globs of oil.

Still, Batumi is worth a visit if only to duck into one of the many restaurants specializing in *adzharuli khachapuri,* the Adzharian version of Georgia's ubiquitous cheese bread. This is my favorite way to eat *khachapuri,* with the yeast bread forming an open boat awash with cheese and butter. Using the crust as both trencher and fork, the diner tears off the pointed ends of the loaf to dip in the near-liquid center.

Coastal Georgians enjoy spicy foods, but the incendiary center of Georgian cuisine lies somewhat farther to the north and east, in the provinces of Imereti, Samegrelo, and Guria. Here the rolling green hills of the Georgian heartland soothe both the eye and spirit. From the west, the littoral reaches gradually give way to foothills dotted with the picturesque remains of ancient churches. From the opposite direction, the geographic contrast is even more striking as the dusty brown heights of the Likhi Range suddenly burst forth into lush forests at the mountain crest, due to the high rainfall on the westward side. Here lies the gateway to western Georgia, once guarded by the Surami fortress, now in ruins. A stream of crystalline water still flows out from under one of the fortress walls. Legend has it that these are the tears of a Georgian lad immured alive in the wall to strengthen it.

The region's hub is the city of Kutaisi, in the province of Imereti. Until the 1920s, when thousands of Georgians flocked to Tbilisi, Kutaisi was the most Georgian of Georgian cities. It remains less ethnically mixed than the capital. Straddling the Rioni River, Kutaisi enjoyed considerable strategic importance and served as the capital of western Georgia from the eighth to the nineteenth centuries. Although now a provincial city, it is still long on charm, with a thriving market-place and a landscape like the Hollywood hills.

Not far from Kutaisi are the famous caverns of Mount Sataplia, where billions of wild bees once swarmed (the name comes from the Georgian word for honey, *tapli*). The trade in honey and wax was of great economic importance to the Kutaisi region, although in the seventeenth century the Turkish traveler Evliya Çelebi (Efendi) warned against the consumption of local honey:

> [They] have a strange mode of burying their Begs [lords]; they put the body into a wooden coffin, which they nail on to the branches of some high tree and make a hole in the coffin near the head, that the Beg, as they say, may look up to Heaven: bees enter the coffin and make honey, entirely wrapping the body up in it; when the season comes they open the coffin, take the honey and sell it, much caution, therefore, is required to be used in purchasing the honey of [these people].
>
> —from *Narrative of Travels in Europe,*
> *Asia and Africa in the Seventeenth Century*

Such a custom may seem extreme, but a little aging can be benefi-cial for certain foods. Western Georgians make an excellent honey vodka, *taplis araki,* by infusing the spirits with honeycombs and letting them mature considerably, while in Guria province slightly rotten wal-nuts are pounded into a particularly pungent sauce.

To the south of Kutaisi is the village of Bagdadi, where the great Russian revolutionary poet Vladimir Mayakovsky was born. Although his family moved to Moscow when he was a child, Mayakovsky re-tained a deep interest in Georgian culture. In one poem, he uses the metaphor of *machari* (new wine) in his call for societal fomentation:

> We are in ferment,
> We
> are
> not yet wine,
> We are still
> just *machari.*
>
> —from "Vladikavkaz-Tiflis" (1924)

One wonders whether Mayakovsky would be offended at how romantic his birthplace appears today, the garden abloom and fragrant with the hundreds of roses planted after his death. Flowers thrive in this soil that has been enriched for centuries by plentiful deposits from the Rioni River and its tributaries. The fluvial reaches of the Kutaisi region also provide an excellent habitat for wildfowl. Pheasant, for one, is indigenous to western Georgia, as its Latin name, *Phasianus colchicus,* attests (the ancients called the Rioni River the Phasis).

North of Kutaisi and Mount Sataplia lies Tskhaltubo, famed for its mineral waters used in the treatment of sterility. Nearby, too, is the popular balneological resort of Sairme. Georgians have long touted the healthful properties of their local mineral waters, such as Sairme and Borzhomi. Russians have also flocked to Georgia's spas to drink and soak in the restorative waters, particularly since 1825, when the pioneer thermochemist Germain Henri Hess published his important study of the medicinal action of mineral waters.

*Taking the waters at the Yevgeniev mineral spring in Borzhomi.*

As the road heads north from Kutaisi, it quickly narrows and steepens, leaving behind the temperate valley zones. Georgia encompasses several mountain provinces in the southern Caucasus range, including Khevi, Tusheti, Pshavi, Mtiuleti, and Khevsureti in the east, and Racha and Svaneti in the west. Most of the mountain peoples raise sheep for meat, cheese, and wool, but they also manage to cultivate fields on a gradient of over twelve percent by carving terraces into the mountainsides. In their isolation, the mountaineers still live simply, proudly wearing their distinctive clothing—the *nabadi,* a warm, waterproof felt cape, and the *papakha,* a high, conical sheepskin hat.

The steep, winding road from Kutaisi to the province of Svaneti seems to go on forever, its sole destination the small town of Mestia, from which the only retreat is by precipitous descent back down the same highway. Dotting the valley and the mountainsides are stone towers, necessary in medieval times to the defense of every household. Quaint and fairytale-like as these crumbling structures appear, life in dark, dank towers must have been grim indeed as families holed up for weeks on end, barricaded as a last refuge against enemy attack. Perhaps because of their successful self-defense, the Svans are blond-haired and blue-eyed, surrounded by swarthy peoples on all sides. Some insist that the Svans are the original Georgians, protected from incursion and intermarriage by the inaccessibility of their region.

Poking my head into Mestia's single store, I found only one variety of preserved goods on the shelves, endlessly repeating itself: pickled *ekala* (sarsaparilla). More than in other parts of Georgia, the people of Svaneti have always had to be self-reliant, eating mainly what they themselves can produce, but it is testimony to the Georgians' intrepid sense of taste that even the mountain dwellers enjoy lively foods. One of the specialties of Svaneti is *kubdari,* bread stuffed with minced meat, often kid. In both Svaneti and nearby Racha province, bear is abundant and considered a good preventive against rheumatism. Rachians also enjoy *mkhali,* a purée of nettles, and *lori,* a special air-dried pork not unlike prosciutto. Complementing the *lori* might be a bottle of Khvanchkara wine, the grapes for which grow on only one river bank in Racha. Despite its severe climate and the resulting agricultural limitations, Racha is said to produce the best Georgian chefs, such as Longinoz Stazhadze, who cooked for Stalin. Stazhadze must be credited with the ingenuity of Odysseus, since he managed to survive the Stalinist purges, eventually becoming the first chef of Moscow's famed Georgian restaurant, Aragvi.

Inevitably, a certain romance attaches to the mountain dwellers of Georgia. Georgia has more documented centenarians than any other country, although skeptics contend that the statistics are misleading, since many Georgians falsified their birth certificates under Stalin in order to avoid forced exile. More intriguing are the claims by various researchers that one group or another is descended from the Lost Tribes of Israel or the Crusaders. This last claim continues to titillate: Not only is the native costume of the stunning horsemen of Khevsureti made of chain mail, it also features a large cross across the chest. And no one can dispute the equestrian skills of these mountaineers. News of their superior horsemanship reached even as far as the United States, and in the 1890s Buffalo Bill Cody invited fifteen Georgian horsemen to tour with his Wild West Congress of Rough Riders. The Ringling Brothers imported another group of horseback riders, including women, to perform in their circus.

*Making butter in a log churn in the village of Mukhrani near Tiflis.*

The eastern mountain provinces are linked with the rest of Georgia as well as with Russia by the Georgian Military Highway, which serves as the main means of transportation and communication. All along the road are panoramic views and scenic villages. One such village is Pasa-nauri, at the confluence of the two Aragvi rivers, the Black and the White. Until the rivers finally mingle, they run within the same banks for a stretch, and the effect of their contrasting colors is striking. More people come to Pasanauri to eat than to gaze at the water, however. The town is a mecca for connoisseurs of *khinkali*, the Georgian version of the boiled dumplings found throughout Central Asia and the Ori-ent. Some claim the special quality of the river waters makes Pasanauri *khinkali* so good; others believe the local flour makes the difference. Whatever the secret, the dumplings are the best appreciated legacy of the Mongol occupation.

Another confluence occurs at the town of Mtskheta, where the Aragvi and Kura rivers meet under a mountain, on top of which rises the magnificent Dzhvari, the Cathedral of the Cross. Even before Christianity was introduced, the Georgians chose this spot to worship their god Armazi, who spread the sun's rays to give plants life. The connection between land and spirit was reaffirmed when the cathedral was built; its floors were laid so that the cracks between stones would resemble plaited vines.

Before the founding of Tbilisi, Mtskheta was the capital of Iberia or eastern Georgia, and like Tbilisi, it boasted considerable natural riches. Although no stories of ready-cooked pheasants from Mtskheta have come down in legend, as late as the nineteenth century Alexandre Dumas praised the region for its poultry and trout. And Lev Tolstoy raved about the bountiful environment: "The hunting is wonderful! Open fields, marshes full of hares, and islands, not of woods but of reeds, where foxes are to be found."

Mtskheta and Tbilisi are only twelve miles apart on the final stretch of the Military Highway. All along this connecting road are tucked churches and picturesque houses, some for escaping the heat of the city, others for year-round living. This central, highly populated prov-ince of Georgia is called Kartli, after the legendary giant Kartlos, a direct descendant of Noah's son Japheth, and father of the Georgian people. Kartlos lent his name to the entire Georgian kingdom, which the Georgians call Sakartvelo, or "the Land of the Karts." (Forms of the name Georgia, by which most of the world knows the nation, may derive from the original Greek *georgos,* "those who work the land.")

Ever since its inception, Tbilisi has been the most important city in Kartli, strategically located in the narrow gorge of the Kura River, which flows from Turkey to the Caspian Sea. At first merely a fortress and castle, the city grew up on the bluffs overlooking the river. Its two halves, the older oriental quarter and the newer western districts, are connected by the Metekhi Bridge at the narrowest point in the gorge. After one particularly bloody battle, both sides of this bridge were lined with the heads of martyred Christians on stakes, a cruel lesson to the surviving residents of the city.

Because of its confining topography, Tbilisi did not spread for many years. Only recently has modern engineering allowed growth into the steep hillsides surrounding the city. Unfortunately, the swelling population and increased number of vehicles have given rise to problems with smog, which does not readily escape the river valley. But the landscape remains dramatic through the haze, and the historical commingling of East and West is still palpable. Today's visitor can easily imagine Tbilisi as one French traveler saw it at the end of the nineteenth century:

At the present day Tiflis is a hybrid town, half Russian and half Oriental. In the centre of it the victors have built a palace, a museum, barracks, boulevards lined with hotels and shops, which vie with those of Moscow. The moment you return to the faubourgs you find yourself in the East again. In the narrow tortuous streets are to be seen the native industries . . . Here the jewellers, working in the open air, in their little stalls, at a bench, where they set turquoises in silver filigree; there the sword cutlers and gunsmiths, squatting in their niches behind a heap of iron, invite you to buy old Persian shields, Khorassan blades, poniards of niello-work from Trebizond, long Kourd guns with the stocks inlaid with mother-of-pearl. Beneath the damp vaults of the bazars, Armenian clerks unfold the silks and gauzes of Asia Minor and carpets from Kirman and Bokhara, piled up in heaps on the floor of a back shop, where the Persian dealer smiles at you in his dyed beard . . .

You go back into the street, and your carriage is stopped by a team of camels, which sway along or kneel down beneath their heavy burden of bales of cotton. Drivers and passers talk back at each other in all languages. The camels draw off to one side to give passage to a Tcherkess horseman, who manages with graceful ease his thorough-bred Kabarda. A Tatar is going to the bathhouse mounted on his donkey; he fingers his chaplet and amber beads as he passes near a pope, who is bargaining for a silver-gilt icon in front of a goldsmith's window. A Russian officer, correctly buttoned up in his green tunic, stares out of countenance the Georgian women who glide along like phantoms—Christians whom long accustomedness has fashioned to Mussulman manners. They are enveloped in long white veils hanging down from a velvet cap worn over the long black braids of hair that frame the sculptural lines of their faces and their great black eyes, whose brilliancy is heightened by the dull paleness of their complexions.

—Vicomte Eugène Melchior de Vogüé,
"Through the Caucasus" (1890)

Vestiges of this oriental city exist today in Tbilisi's Old Town, with its cobbled, twisting streets and carefully restored buildings. The most famous caravansary still stands in Sioni Street, providing even the modern visitor respite from the city's heat and bustle. The façade is European but the interior is traditional, with a large central courtyard and pool around which run three immense stories of galleries. Once the lower floor held warehouses and stables, the main floor shops, the upper floor rooms for the merchants. Today the caravansary houses the State Museum of History and Ethnography as well as a pleasant café where you can sip Turkish coffee or ice cream sodas. Tbilisi continues to teeter between East and West.

Not far from the caravansary are the fabled Tiflis baths, the site of Gorgaslani's lucky find. The baths are recognizable only by the slight smell of sulphur in the air and the beehive domes projecting into the street. The baths are subterranean, a marvel of marble and stone illuminated by the domed ceilings. At one time these chambers were the scene of much more than cleansing. Business deals and matchmaking were regularly carried out in the pools and steam rooms, and the expansive vestibules held many a lavish feast. In the seventeenth century Evliya Çelebi reported that "sheeps' heads and feet are cooked . . . in a hot springs [that] boils out of the ground without the assistance of fire." And nearly two hundred years later, the Russian poet Pushkin related this experience in the Tiflis baths, for which he uses no alternate persona nor poetic license:

At the entrance to the baths sat the proprietor, an old Persian man. He opened the door for me, I entered a spacious room, and what did I see? More than fifty women, young and old, half-dressed and completely naked, sitting and standing, undressing and dressing on the benches lining the walls. I stood stock still.

"Come on, come on," said my host, "today's Tuesday: ladies' day! It's nothing, no problem."

"Of course it's no problem," I answered, "quite the contrary." . . . Many of them were in fact very beautiful, justifying Thomas Moore's imagination:

> a lovely Georgian maid,
> With all the bloom, the freshen'd glow
> Of her own country maiden's looks,
> When warm they rise from Teflis' brooks.

. . . Never in my life have I encountered in Russia or in Turkey anything more sumptuous than the Tiflis baths.

—Alexander Pushkin,
*Journey to Arzrum* (1835)

Alexandre Dumas describes a similar experience in the Tiflis baths, claiming embarrassment from the women's lack of modesty. Yet in another tale from the Tiflis baths he presents modesty as a folly, not a virtue. Dumas recounts the fate of an Armenian archbishop too modest to allow the regular bath attendants to supervise him in the steam room. Instead he orders his own deacons to hold the four corners of a large towel suspending him over a bath of near-boiling mineral waters. Whether from inexperience or the archbishop's weight, one of the deacons loses hold of his corner, sending the archbishop straight into the water. By the time the bath attendants could extract him, the archbishop was already done for. As Dumas explains with a certain culinary wit: *"Il était trop tard. Monseigneur était cuit."* ("He was too late. Monseigneur was cooked.") The pheasant, the archbishop. History repeats itself first in tragedy, then in farce.

Tbilisi still surprises the visitor with serendipity. After passing numerous dull, Soviet-style establishments, you'll suddenly find yourself in a shop specializing in Eastern sweets that seems straight out of *The Arabian Nights*. Its walls and ceiling are finished entirely in mirrors covered by intricately carved and painted wooden fretwork, the mirrored facets reflecting a thousand times the mounds of halvah, sugared nuts, and meringues in the display cases—a legacy of Islamic rule. Another favorite spot is Mitrofan Lagidze's parlor for sparkling *tsklebi* or fruit drinks, founded early in this century. Here, the thirsty patron chooses from a variety of syrups in brilliant hues—emerald *tarkhuna*

*The famous buffet in Tiflis's Paliashvili Opera House.*

or tarragon, ruby *khakhuri* or wine-flavored, canary *kolkhida* or citrus
—mixed with carbonated water for a bracing drink.

Tbilisi's busy *meidani* or market square, once ablaze with the
colorful costumes and wares of many nations, is now a pedestrian mall.
Here shoppers can admire the local crafts: beautiful chased copper and
brassware; distinctive black-glazed pottery; intricately fashioned niello-
work; silver jewelry inlaid with turquoise and onyx; and heavy felt
rugs with bright geometric designs. Tbilisi has a rich tradition of
public music, with one of the oldest opera houses in the East. Indeed,
the city's atmosphere seems inspired by Euterpe. Tchaikovsky began
composing two of his greatest works in Tbilisi, *The Sleeping Beauty*
and *The Queen of Spades*. And the great operatic bass Fyodor Chaliapin
exclaimed: "I was born twice: in Kazan I opened my eyes to life and
in Tbilisi—to music."

In Tbilisi, many nationalities live side by side. In addition to Georgians, the city has long been home to Armenians, Persians, Kurds, Jews, Greeks, and Russians. Even today, an active mosque and synagogue stand within just a few blocks of the Georgian Orthodox Cathedral, witness to the heterogeneous population. For years the commercial life of the city was supported by Armenians, successful tradespeople who actually dominated the population until fairly recently. The Georgians preferred a less hectic life that enabled them to return frequently to their rural, ancestral villages to renew ties with friends and family and commune with the source of their wine and food. But although the Armenian presence was certainly felt, in the culinary realm it had surprisingly little effect. There is no significant interplay between Georgian and Armenian cuisines, the Armenian being much closer to Turkish and Persian in both substance and method. Only such dishes as *khashi* (tripe soup), *bozbashi* (lamb soup), *borani* (vegetables with yogurt), *lavashi* (thin bread), *nazuki* (spice bread), and *gozinaki* (candied nuts) share a common vocabulary and a mutual appeal.

At the edge of Tbilisi's old quarter once lay the famous Ortachala Gardens, now engulfed by urban sprawl. These pleasure gardens tempted visitors with restaurants bearing such fanciful names as "Eldorado," "Fantasia," and "Gentleman." It was here that the Georgian primitivist painter Pirosmani (Niko Pirosmanashvili) spent much of his time, listening to the cabaret songs of his beloved Margarita. Self-taught and penurious, Pirosmani kept himself alive by painting signboards on black oilcloth, tin, and scavenged pieces of wood for Tbilisi's many taverns and shops. By 1912, Pirosmani's fanciful figures could be seen throughout the city. Tavern patrons enjoyed a skewer of *mtsvadi* or shish-kebab under a Pirosmani painting of diners reveling at an al fresco feast. His still lifes read like menus of tavern fare: *mtsvadi,* barbel (a local fish), suckling pig, chicken, sausage, fruits, scallions, radishes, and cucumbers all line up in a row, begging the viewer's selection. Pirosmani presented food in its unadorned simplicity, its most essential form. Dominated by the colors of the fruits of the earth—the yellow of grain and the red of wine—his canvases often portray the trinity of bread, wine, and salt.

The tavernkeepers scarcely appreciated Pirosmani's art, rewarding his labors meagerly with a bowl of soup and a bottle of wine. Even after Pirosmani was discovered in 1912 by the Zdanevich brothers Ilya and Kirill, artists who brought his work to the attention of the Russian avant-garde, he did not change his style of living, but continued to dwell in a damp wine warehouse, hastening his early death in 1918. In the meantime, Russia had entered World War I, and war concerns dampened the activities of avant-garde literary and artistic groups in Moscow and Petrograd. Georgia, no longer a place of exile, now represented a haven, and Tbilisi began to emerge as a center of modernist activity. A group of talented Georgian poets, the "Blue Horns," frequently held readings and lively discussions in the city's many coffeehouses and cafés. One of the best places to see the avant-garde in action was at the "Fantastic Little Tavern," where the walls were decorated with murals by the painters Lado Gudiashvili, David Kakabadze, and Sergei Sudeikin. A second café favored by the avant-garde was "Chimaera." At both places patrons could enjoy a bowl of *kharcho,* a spicy beef soup with tomatoes and aromatic herbs.

Despite seventy years of stifling Soviet rule—now, happily, a thing of the past—Tbilisi still has a lively urban scene in which cafés feature prominently. On warm evenings Tbilisians like to take the funicular, the longest and steepest in the world, up the slopes of Mount Mtatsminda, which rises over the Kura River. There were once so many *dukani*s or taverns at the top that Ostap Bender, the hero of Ilf and Petrov's *The Twelve Chairs,* called it "Restaurant Mountain." Today Mtatsminda is a family gathering place, its single huge restaurant affording a panoramic view of the city below. Particularly striking are the houses hugging the river banks in the old part of the city. They cling to the craggy cliffs of the river like so many swallows' nests, their balconies precariously cantilevered out over the water.

Tbilisi is known as a city of balconies, and these ornately carved railings, pillars, and canopies lend a fanciful air to otherwise unremarkable flat-roofed dwellings. As in San Francisco, the steep, winding streets of the old town often end suddenly in a flight of steps leading directly onto a balcony, which must be traversed to reach the next street level. The balconies of these old houses are vital to the Georgian way of life. Unlike in San Francisco, they are not private, but communal, running the length of several houses and reached by exterior stairs from the street. Since balconies are often larger than the interior rooms, they serve for both eating and sleeping during hot summer nights. But most important, they encourage impromptu gatherings and celebrations.

*A balconied house in Tbilisi hugging the cliffs over the Kura River.*

For the Russian poet Boris Pasternak, Tbilisi shimmered hypnotically, seemingly unnatural in its natural setting—man's creation in a still wild realm:

> It so completely mocked the sphere
> Of the eye's range and all of nature,
> That it arose and remained a chimaera,
> A city as if not of this world.

Pasternak's lines capture a certain otherworldly air in Tbilisi, but to escape this dream realm all the visitor need do is take a bite of the local *khachapuri* to feel the city's visceral connection to this earth.

An old road heads out of Tbilisi to the east, following the ancient trade route. This road leads to the province of Kakheti, winding over the beautiful Gombori Pass before descending into the fertile Alazani Valley. Because Kakheti is home to Georgia's wine industry, this highway is commonly known as "The Grape Trail." In the broad lowlands along the Alazani River lies prime wine country, set off by the stark, snow-capped peaks of the Caucasus rising in the distance. Summers are long and hot, winters mild. The largest city in Kakheti is Telavi, its modern thoroughfares seeming anomalous next to the crenellated walls of King Irakli II's castle and the magnificent eight-hundred-year-old plane tree that graces the center of town. The spirit of Kakheti is better preserved in its villages, which adjoin one another in a corridor designed to protect against invasion.

We stayed for a few days in the village of Velistsikhe, which seems to belong to an old and almost forgotten world, with its narrow streets fronted on all sides by high stone walls plastered with mud. Throughout the Kahketian countryside are similar village compounds. On every promontory or rise the ruins of citadels and fortresses stand over the populace below. Our hosts in Velistsikhe were Bichiko and Dodo and their daughter Tamriko. When Bichiko opened the heavy metal gates set into the wall fronting his house, I was surprised to see such a spacious courtyard after the cramped confines of the street. As with other Georgian houses, the most prominent feature of this one was the large, second-story veranda running the length of the house, a place to escape the searing heat of summer. Although it was nearly midnight, we immediately sat down to tea with an assortment of Dodo's wonderful homemade preserves: whole peaches suspended in sugar syrup, with a suggestion of cinnamon and clove; crunchy slices of spiced watermelon rind; aromatic rose-petal jam shimmering in its bowl; and the favorite Georgian green walnut preserve, lush and ambrosial. Gazing around the house and yard, we were delighted by the juxtaposition of old and new. At the far end of the yard was a shed housing an old-fashioned *toné* or clay bake oven; next to it, a garage holding Bichiko's late-model car. Though the house had no indoor plumbing, the dining room boasted a window air conditioner. At this hour, though, we sat on the veranda to enjoy the gentle night.

The next morning we rose early to watch Dodo make bread in the *toné*. After starting a fire with dried grape vines, she brought out the dough she had mixed the night before. Soon a neighbor appeared to help with the baking. Unlike Dodo, who wore a light, sleeveless frock, seemingly indifferent to the hazards of baking, the neighbor was dressed entirely in black, from the scarf reaching halfway down her forehead to the fingerless gloves she wore to protect her hands from the oven's intense heat. Now the activity began, a series of rhythmic movements as the women worked in harmony, shaping the loaves, slapping them onto the sides of the oven, spearing them once they'd turned crusty and brown, then turning them out onto a board to cool. Their graceful, repetitive motions were mesmerizing, as were the smells of wood smoke and fresh bread. But Bichiko was eager to show us his orchard, so while the breadbaking continued, we dashed off to pick fresh fruits for breakfast. Bichiko's plot lay on the outskirts of town, a brief car ride away, in a public area set aside for individual gardens. While some of the gardens seemed overgrown or haphazard, Bichiko's was a model of tidiness, with virtually every square foot under intensive cultivation. Here grew several varieties of peaches, apricots, plums, and summer apples, as well as red and white grapes and tomatoes. Bichiko beamed and pointed as we harvested buckets full of sweet plums, rosy peaches, and apricots with the dew still clinging to them. Racing back in time to enjoy the bread still warm from the oven, we savored homemade yogurt, cheese, and olives along with our fruit.

In contrast to the spiciness of western Georgian food, eastern Georgian cooking is subtle, relying on combinations of fresh ingredients and spare seasonings. This Kakhetian breakfast highlighted all that is best about the way Georgians eat—their excitement over seasonal produce, the absolute freshness of their food, the simplicity of much of its preparation. But splendid as the meal was, the memory that remains with me most vividly is of two bent old women working so skillfully around the *toné*. In another setting, these women might have seemed unremarkable, but here, intent upon a task that generations of Georgians had performed before them, they became models of grace, priestesses tending a sacred fire. The force of the *toné*'s heat was staggering—pure and elemental. With the craggy mountains looming in the distance, the spirit of Prometheus seemed surely alive.

*A troupe of traditional Tiflis musicians.*

# 2

# The Georgian Feast

T he Russian poet Alexander Pushkin once commented that every
Georgian dish is a poem. High praise, indeed! Pushkin likely
appreciated not only the transcendent flavors of Georgian
foods, but also the fervor with which they are savored. Georgians display passion in both the preparation and consumption of a
meal. And to the uninitiated, a Georgian feast or *supra* can be over-
whelming, with its rituals prescribed by centuries of tradition.

Many first-time visitors are unaware that participation at the Georgian table calls for the skillful exercise of moderation in the face of
excess. This is no small feat, considering the courtesies and extrava-
gances of the meal. One memorable feast I attended took place in the
small town of Khobi in western Georgia. Our hosts were Guram and
Gulisa Lataria and their twelve-year-old son Goga. As manager and
part owner of a large tea-processing plant, Guram had a keen nose for
fine aromas and tastes, and his wife was a legendary cook. While
Guram seated us with the other guests, Gulisa scurried between
kitchen and dining room. She had set a dazzling table. Spread along
its entire length was a colorful array of dishes: cabbage, carrot, and
eggplant slices stuffed with an aromatic mixture of walnuts, spices, and
pomegranate seeds; two different kinds of *khachapuri* or cheese bread,
one open-faced like a pizza, the other enclosed in an envelope of yeast
dough; chicken *satsivi*, roasted then topped with a sauce of ground
walnuts; boiled kid; and *gomi*, the Georgian version of grits. We had
hardly managed to fill our plates when Gulisa brought in a steaming

bowl of *gadazelili khveli,* fresh mozzarellalike cheese boiled briefly in milk, then poured out onto a plate and kneaded with mint leaves. To cleanse our palates, Gulisa next offered bowls of fresh hazelnuts, fruits, and smoky honey. We continued to indulge, punctuating mouthfuls with toasts and Guram's homemade red wine. Late into the feasting, plates of hot, half-moon-shaped cheese dumplings were passed around. Then we ate more fruit, this time watermelon and a sort of honeydew, along with squares of wonderful *pelamushi,* grape juice that has been thickened with cornmeal. Sated beyond all limits, we still could not offend our hosts by declining to sample the boiled corn on the cob and squash offered next. A huge fruit cake, two feet in diameter and topped with confectionery lilies, signaled the end of the feast —and nearly the end of us.

*Ornate confections from a Kutaisi bakery.*

What made this meal unforgettable, apart from the savory food and surfeit, was the timing of our visit. We had arrived in western Georgia from Turkey under the protective wing of our old friend Zaza. Only a few miles outside of Khobi, however, the radio announced that ethnic riots had erupted just to our north. This report made Zaza understandably anxious. We suggested that it might be better not to impose on his friends in Khobi at such a difficult time.

But we had misunderstood Zaza's anxiety. He was fretting that the political instability would prevent him from doing justice to us, his honored guests. When we arrived in Khobi, Guram and Gulisa were visibly upset, but they made it clear that their concern arose not from any sense of inconvenience, as we expected, but again from a fear that they might not be able to regale us properly. After all, Georgian tradition demands that guests be accorded due honor, and a feast must inevitably ensue. So that evening we went out to watch the frightening specter of Soviet tanks rolling through the town, then returned home to our spectacular feast. The experience was instructive: for Georgians, neither food nor nationalism is a trivial concern.

Such hospitality can seem burdensome if you are tired and want nothing more than a bite and bed. Numerous visitors to Georgia tell of arriving bone-tired only to find that a sheep has to be slaughtered and grilled in their honor. Refusing such a feast would be an insult, so certain sumptuous rigors must be endured. Odette Keun, an intrepid Frenchwoman who traveled to Georgia in the early 1920s, found her effusive reception an ordeal:

> My disgusted orderly officer presented me as a European without endurance and without manners, but he condescended to ask the *tamada,* the president of the banquet, to allow me to retire at a certain hour. Social conventions are a perfect tyranny among the Georgians; I have been *martyrized* in my travels by their inexorable notions of propriety; the British themselves are not more ferocious on this point. Again and again I have arrived half dead at a village, tortured by a bad saddle, devoured by lice, galled by my masculine riding costume, asking only to be allowed to eat a bite of bread and drink some tea, so that I might wash and lie down immediately, and I have been made to wait, perched on a hard chair for hours—it would have appeared rude to stretch myself out—while they prepared a feast. I laugh now when I recall all the tears of exasperation that these attentions cost me, but at the time I did not feel at all hilarious. When I had dismounted, it is true they would offer me maize cakes and tea; but when I spoke of going to bed, I would learn, to my unspeakable horror, that they had gone to kill a sheep.
>
> —from *In the Land of the Golden Fleece*

If guests arrive at a home unexpectedly when no food is on hand, one's neighbors will rally to offer provisions from their own larders, knowing that the gesture will be reciprocated in time. Like the ancient Greeks, Georgians sincerely believe that hospitality is akin to godliness, and that failure to honor a guest is a serious transgression. Even today Georgians take to heart the words of their great twelfth-century poet Shota Rustaveli:

> Spending on feasting and wine is better than
> hoarding our substance.
> That which we give makes us richer, that
> which is hoarded is lost.
> —from *The Knight in the Panther's Skin*

Feasting means more than just honoring guests, however. The shared table serves to promote a feeling of kinship and national unity. In a sense, entering Georgia is like entering a kingdom that still lives by ancient codes. Centuries of gathering around the table to affirm their traditions have helped the Georgians preserve their culture even under foreign subjugation. The *supra* or laid table represents the public face the Georgians proudly present to the world; it reflects the honor of each household. Ritual celebrations, both great and small, take place around the family table. And the rules for the celebration are strict.

Most important, a *tamada* or toastmaster is chosen to orchestrate all feasts but the most informal. This position is taken very seriously and accorded great respect, for it requires skill to keep all the guests entertained, ensure that the meal is proceeding apace, and see to it that no one drinks or eats to excess—drunken guests bring shame on the host. If the gathering is small, the host himself will typically serve as *tamada,* but for a large company the *tamada,* like a godfather, is chosen from outside the family. The role is always filled by a man, most often an elder who knows most of the people present. The best *tamadas* are renowned for their wit and eloquence, including an ability to improvise. Even though they must adhere to ritual form, they strive through verbal pyrotechnics to make each feast seem new and exciting so that the guests are not bored.

Until the early part of this century, training schools for *tamadas* existed in Tbilisi, but more recently the art has been passed on through observation. The *tamada* guides the company through a series of toasts, which can be brief or complex, depending on the theme and the *tamada*'s inclination. Each toast calls for downing a glass of wine. Georgians do not sip, and drinking out of order or at random is not allowed. A *merikipe* is appointed to make sure that diners' glasses are filled at all times. To monitor wine consumption, Georgians prefer crystal glasses that reveal when the wine has been drained. Guests will often turn their empty glasses upside down to emphasize completion of a toast, murmuring "May you be emptied of enemies as this glass has been emptied of wine."

The rules of the Georgian table call for uplifting toasts; each occasion, even a sad one, becomes an affirmation of life. Traditionally, toasting begins with glasses raised to the ceiling in acknowledgment of God's presence. Then the host family is toasted, particularly the lady of the house, responsible for the meal. (If the *tamada* is from outside the family, the host may briefly toast him first.) Then parents, children, guests, and those absent are remembered in succession. With each toast, another glass of wine is drained. Often the *tamada*'s words are seconded by others in the gathering, who rise to say a few words about a parent or friend. If the *tamada* knows that one of the guests has something particularly appropriate or moving to say, he may offer that person *alaverdi,* permission to pronounce the next toast. Here the *tamada*'s sensitivity is especially important as he surveys those gathered around the table, making sure that everyone is included and given an opportunity to speak. In this way the feast is an exercise in democratic form, with a strong executive branch.

The *tamada*'s ability to pace the evening is also crucial. Each time a toast is pronounced, whether by the *tamada* or another person, wine is drunk as a mark of honor. But if inebriation seems likely, the *tamada* must slow down the succession of toasts. And so the evening proceeds. After a toast to Georgia ("*Sakartvelos gaumardzhos!*"), the themes often grow more abstract as the speakers wax poetic on love and friendship, health and beauty. At least at the feast table, every Georgian is a poet, and competition can turn the meal into a celebration not only of the occasion but of the oratory art.

One especially eloquent toast is memorialized in a poem by the Georgian Romantic Grigol Orbeliani, written on the occasion of the battle of Yerevan. This toast begins by honoring all those who have fallen in defense of their homeland. The poem's *tamada* then travels through history, enumerating Georgia's past rulers and their accomplishments, from King Farnavazi, who introduced the alphabet, to Levan, the last brave scion of the Bagrationi dynasty. The revelers drink, in turn, to Miriani, who embraced Christianity for his nation;

to Gorgaslani, the Georgian King Arthur; to David, peacemaker and builder of a united Georgia; to Tamara, great queen of the Renaissance; to Ketevan, the martyr who chose imprisonment over acceptance of Islam; to Vakhtangi, judicious lawgiver; and to Irakli, who bravely fought for Georgia's independence. Declaring that "we love our country more than life," the revelers reaffirm their common history and devotion to their land.

Though less elaborate than Orbeliani's, toasts at contemporary feasts continue to serve as a medium for airing politics and relationships. Like members of a social club, the participants carry on a "conversation" that is given structure by the *tamada*. No matter what the individual variations, however, the toasting usually ends with the *qovel-tatsminda*, a final round to all that is holy. In this way the Georgians begin and end their festivities with words of thanks, the toasting serving as a sacrament of sorts.

With the large number of toasts governed by tradition, it might appear impossible to drink temperately at a Georgian feast. But since the Georgians regularly attend such gatherings (any happening, no matter how trivial, can be a pretext), they know the tricks of moderation. For one thing, they never imbibe wine without food, which is continuously brought to table throughout the meal. In eating, too, Georgians show restraint and pace themselves: Plenitude is not cause for gluttony. Most feasts begin around eight o'clock in the evening, after the participants have already had a snack at home. It is not considered good form to arrive ravenous.

The traditional meal is punctuated by breaks in the toasting for entertainment as well as respite, a holdover from medieval patterns of feasting when entremets were actually diversions. Georgians are noted for their a capella harmonies, and men who have sung together for years will often break into song when conversation flags. At formal feasts, musicians at one time were hired to greet the guests and accompany the meal. These musicians, in native costume, played such old Georgian string and wind instruments as the *zurna, daira, tari,* and *sazi,* resembling clarinet, tambourine, banjo, and lute. Today the accompaniment is more likely a guitar, to which men and women alike will dance around the table. After this necessary period of relaxation and exercise, the company once again focuses on the table as eating and drinking resume.

Given the ritual forms of drinking, it may seem surprising that there is no prescribed order of courses. To an American, the Georgian table can appear chaotic, but the service is actually designed both to dazzle the eye and pique the palate through contrasting colors, textures, and flavors. When diners sit down to eat, the table is already laid with a wide variety of dishes. Many of these foods have been prepared well in advance, a boon for the hostess, since traditional preparations demand time and patience. (Food processors and other kitchen aids are still extremely rare.) Happily, Georgians prefer most foods at room temperature, so that flavors are not subdued by too much heat or cold.

Several of the dishes initially placed on the table contain fresh or cooked vegetables, the glory of Georgian cuisine. Mounds of bread—baton-shaped *shoti* or half-moon-shaped *puri*—grace both ends of the board. Each diner's place is set with a small plate and several glasses. As the evening progresses, new foods are brought out to supplement, not replace, the old. Some of these are hot and meant to be eaten right away, such as *elardzhi,* steaming grits mixed with cheese, served in near-liquid form, or *chakhokhbili,* an aromatic chicken stew. The hostess does not remove serving plates that still contain food, but rather continues to pile new dishes on the table, balancing some on the edges of others, so that by the end of the evening the table is laden with a pyramid of plates, ensuring plenty at every stage. The diners' plates are regularly and assiduously removed, however, and new flatware frequently distributed, so that incompatible flavors are not mixed on the plate or bones left staring the diner in the face as a reminder of the chicken polished off hours before.

A typical feast for birthday, anniversary, or nameday celebrations lasts from four to six hours, so copious amounts of food must be prepared. Rarely does a single cook take on the entire burden. More often friends and family members (generally female) get together and cook for several days in advance, the preparation being as joyous a social occasion as the feast that follows. The foods served vary from season to season and family to family, with the universal proviso that they inspire a sense of abundance and gaiety, even on sad occasions. This deliberate delectation is hyperbolically described by the nineteenth-century French traveler Vicomte Eugène Melchior de Vogüé, who tells how funeral repasts in Georgia celebrate life even as they mourn its loss:

But the supreme pleasure . . . is a fine funeral. . . . The family keeps a corpse, according to the condition and fortune of the deceased, ten, twelve, fifteen days, and even longer: friends from distant parts must have time to put their urgent affairs in order and to arrive at the spot. When a sufficient crowd is gathered in the house of the deceased the tragedy of the funeral begins, a veritable dramatic representation, with hired or voluntary weepers, dialogues, eloquent speeches, and soul-stirring cries, like those of the *vocératrices* of Corsica. When all the actors and orators are tired out, the dead man is buried . . . then the gayety begins around a banquet worthy of Pantagruel. Cattle are slain, buffalo-skins full of wine of Kakhetia are tapped, and eating and drinking continue until the guests roll under the table, that is to say, on the grass, where they squat in front of the victuals . . . People still talk at Zougdidi about the funeral of the Dédophale, the Dowager Princess Dadian who died a few years ago. After waiting three weeks, 80,000 people were assembled in the courts of the castle, and the cries and howlings could be heard for several miles around. The banquet continued for three whole days, and entire herds of oxen and sheep were slaughtered before the roasting spits of the cooks.

—Vicomte Eugène Melchior de Vogüé,
"Through the Caucasus" (1890)

These days, large feasts are more likely to include eighty than eighty thousand guests, but the principles of hospitality and extravagance endure. As the Georgians like to say, "The sun rises on the home visited by a guest. And when the guest leaves, the sun sets on his host."

This sort of exuberant welcome was extended to my husband and me when we visited Givi and Daredzhan Abesadze at their country house in Kursebi, just outside the western Georgian city of Kutaisi. Givi is the owner of a restaurant in Kutaisi, so he works long hours to make his venture a success. Givi was not home when we arrived in Kursebi, chugging and sputtering up the steep and rutted dirt road leading to the Abesadzes' house. As we swerved into their courtyard, scattering chickens in all directions, we encountered a typical western Georgian two-story house. An outdoor staircase provided the only access to the second floor, which had a covered balcony running the length of two sides.

This type of house developed from the earliest dwellings, designed like the tepee with one large room with a hearth in the middle and a large domed opening in the roof, a "window on heaven." Rain notwithstanding, such an opening allowed smoke to go out and light to come in. The hearth occupied both the physical and spiritual center of the home. Supporting the roof dome was a finely carved *dedabodzi* or "mother column," a T-shaped structure that symbolized the relation between earth and sun and protected the house from evil. Early Georgians hung this column with all sorts of food, in both sacrifice and celebration. For practical purposes cheeses were often suspended on it to smoke. Although *dedabodzi*s are now found only in museums, their spirit is still felt in the best of households. This was certainly true at the Abesadzes'.

Greeting us, Daredzhan was all aflutter. Her son was taking university entrance exams that day, and she apologized profusely for having to leave us, but ritual demanded that she go stand for three hours in the hot sun with other anxious mothers, waiting to hear preliminary results. We were left with Givi's mother, a grinning old peasant woman with Popeye arms. As the family matriarch showed us around the property, we felt the truth of the saying that any twig stuck into Georgian soil will grow into a tree, even if it is planted upside down. The proof lay in Givi's orchards and vineyards, a terraced profusion along the steep slope behind the house.

In traditional Georgian homes the front yard is maintained as the "clean" yard for guests, with ornamental flowers and trees. The back yard is meant for household use, and it is here that the serious businesses of gardening, viticulture, and husbandry are conducted. In the Abesadzes' backyard we saw huge *kvevri*s or wine amphoras dug right into the ground for aging the wine Givi made from his grapes. Here, too, were Daredzhan's gardens of strawberries, corn, peppers, tomatoes, and herbs. The Abesadzes were still working on their "clean" yard, and in contrast to the neat rows of vegetables and herbs in the back, the front was in chaos, with chickens, geese, turkeys, and dogs running all about. One of these chickens Givi's mother expeditiously caught, killed, and cleaned for the evening meal.

Like other Georgians who live close to the earth, the Abesadze family celebrates food, taking a special delight in their home-grown produce. Even though Daredzhan hadn't been able to spend hours preparing dinner, as soon as she returned from the university—beaming—we sat down to a meal perfect in its balance of flavors. Givi's mother had flattened the chicken slightly, sprinkled it with salt, and placed it in a heated *ketsi* or red clay dish that she covered with a second hot *ketsi* and set next to an open fire to roast by indirect heat. This succulent chicken was complemented by Daredzhan's own *tkemali* sauce, made from tart plums from the orchard and enlivened with the hot peppers, fennel, garlic, cilantro, and mint she grew in the yard. We also ate *lobio,* green beans puréed by hand with cilantro, basil, walnuts, and a touch of vinegar; and *adzhapsandali,* a fiery medley of eggplant, tomatoes, potatoes, peppers, and fresh herbs. *Khachapuri* and *mchadi,* or corncakes, rounded out the meal.

I was fascinated to watch Givi's mother make *mchadi* in the traditional way. First she started a fire from twigs and branches. While the flames gained momentum she gathered together a number of red-clay *ketsi*s and placed them directly into the fire to heat. Back in the kitchen, she mixed a moist dough of white cornmeal and water, then molded it into several patties. When the *ketsi*s were hot, she placed two or three fresh chestnut leaves on top of each patty and inverted them into the dishes, adding more leaves to impart aroma and prevent burning. She then stacked the hot *ketsi*s five high, leaving an empty dish at the top. The hot clay immediately began to cook the corncakes inside. By this time, the flames had burned down to hot coals, some of which she placed in the empty *ketsi* atop the corncakes. After about fifteen minutes, she tested the *mchadi* in the middle dish by tapping it—unlike our American cornbread, *mchadi*s are not meant to be moist, but neither should they be allowed to dry out. Assured by the hollow knock that the corncakes were ready, she scraped off the soot and carried them steaming into the dining room. Clearly this art was a fine one, requiring an understanding of the fire's heat to estimate cooking time.

To our dismay, Givi's mother refused to join us at table, although she did appear for a toast in her honor. We drank various varietals and vintages, all made from Givi's backyard grapes. Like other wines produced in western Georgia, Givi's were generally lighter and less tannic than the wines we tasted in the eastern region of Kakheti. Givi had to work late, but having learned of his son's success at school, he arrived home soon after dinner carting a fillet of beef and a leg of fresh pork in celebration. He deftly butchered the meat for *mtsvadi* or shish-kebab, alternating it with onions on long sticks used as skewers, and we ate our second supper al fresco on the upstairs balcony, following the moon with surfeited gaze as it rose over the surrounding hills.

This late-night supper, so typical of the spirit of Georgia, showed that every meal, even the most improvised, can be a feast. Zest and reverence for the act of eating are what transform a simple repast into true regalement. Certainly it helps to have snow-capped mountains as backdrop and eat achingly fresh food. But a festive spirit can prevail even in a cramped apartment, as long as the food is shared.

Georgians insist that whoever drinks from the waters of the Kura River will drink from them again, for once the visitor is touched by Georgia's spell he must return. Subsequent visits do not disappoint; neither do they lessen in intensity. As always, tables are laid, goblets filled. Soon all rigors of travel disappear. The ritual of feasting brings us together, creating a spirit of community that binds not only individuals but peoples. To dine with the Georgians and participate in their traditions, engaging the senses with lush colors, eloquent oratory, and savory food, is to relearn something about human nature. And so we leave the Georgian feast with palates sated. Herein lies the strength of the Georgian people, a lesson we could do well to learn: Life is short, celebrate!

*Tiflis shopkeepers with earthenware pots.*

# 3

# The Flavors of Georgia

ituated at the crossroads of East and West, Georgia has endured its share of invasions. But it has also experienced some of the benefits of foreign influence, more visible in gastronomy than in politics. Georgian food is reminiscent of both Mediterranean and Middle Eastern tastes, the result of a rich interplay of culinary ideas carried along the trade routes by merchants and travelers. Yet even as the Georgians embraced new seasonings and methods, they did not blithely adopt all the culinary practices that came their way. Today their cooking represents more than a mélange of the flavors of other regions. Georgian cuisine stands distinct among the foods of the world, a vibrant, inspired interpretation of indigenous ingredients.

Certain outside influences remain easily recognizable, of course. The pilafs of southeastern Georgia, along with the meats stewed with fruit, echo similar dishes in neighboring Iran, while the prized *khinkali* or wontonlike dumplings of the mountainous zones show evidence of Tatar influence. Along the Black Sea coast in western Georgia, the stuffed vegetable *tolma*s resemble Turkey's various *dolma*s. But the Georgians never developed a taste for the elaborate oriental sweets from Turkish, Persian, or Armenian kitchens; instead they limit their desserts mainly to fresh fruits and nut preparations. And even though Georgian cooking nods to Persian by using fruits with meat, it claims as its own only those dishes yielding the tart taste the Georgians prefer. Thus meat is more often stewed with sour plums or pomegranates than with the sweeter quince or prunes.

What is perhaps most interesting (and yet to be fully documented) is the similarity of Georgian food to that of northern India. This is no coincidence, since the foodways of northern India are a legacy of the ruling Mughals, otherwise known as the Central Asian Mongols who left their imprint on Georgia as well. Yet the correspondences in culinary terminology are notable within a language like Georgian, which is not even Indo-European but constitutes a separate linguistic group (South Caucasian). The Georgian word for bread, like the Hindi, is *puri;* and the Georgians use a clay oven, the *toné,* for baking bread and cooking much as Indians of the Punjab use the *tandoor.* The cast-iron skillet or *tava* of northern India is related to the Georgia *tapha,* used for making the succulent chicken *tabaka* that has become emblematic of Georgian cuisine. And curry blends find their counterpart in *khmeli-suneli,* the aromatic herb and spice mixture of Georgia.

But differences always tell more than similarities. And what most distinguishes Georgian cuisine is its use of walnuts—not merely as garnish, but as an integral component of a wide variety of dishes. Georgian cooks have learned how to temper the walnut's oiliness even as they highlight its nuttiness. This balancing act is crucial to the success of any dish, and most recipes call for intricate proportions of ingredients. To offset what might otherwise be a cloying richness from the nuts, many recipes call for the addition of a souring agent to impart a tart taste. Yogurt *(matsoni),* pungent cheese, and immature wine *(machari)* often serve as counterpoints to ground walnuts; vinegar or fruit juices and fruit leathers likewise lend balance. But even though ground walnuts find their way into many dishes, the flavors of Georgian food are not redundant. The various proportions of nuts and spices are carefully calculated to highlight the flavor of whatever basic ingredient is used, whether fish or fowl, dairy product or vegetable.

As it happens, some of the most tempting recipes are for vegetables, which account for the greatest part of the Georgian culinary repertoire. While meat has become commonplace, in daily life the Georgians still prefer plants. This custom derives both from tradition and taste. Until recent times the diet of most Georgians consisted largely of vegetables, dairy products, and bread, meat being a luxury reserved for feast days. Over one hundred varieties of such wild greens as sarsaparilla, nettles, mallow, ramp, and purslane were eagerly gathered in season and prepared in a surprising number of ways—cooked, marinated, dried for seasoning, or steeped in water for a nutritious drink. But above all, the Georgians enjoyed their greens fresh. Even today the Georgian table is incomplete without fresh greens meant for eating out of hand: leafy cilantro, dill, tarragon, parsley, and basil share platters with scallions, summer savory, and peppery *tsitsmati* or false-flax *(Camelina sativa),* similar to arugula. The plants provide nourishment as well as a refreshing counterpoint to the heavier foods in the meal.

Perhaps the most characteristic Georgian flavors are to be found in western Georgia, a place where the food is redolent of earth and sun. Here is the motherlode of Georgian cuisine, thanks to fertile soil and abundant harvests. Western Georgian cooks have turned their bounty to good advantage, developing a varied and sophisticated cuisine. In this region grow the most aromatic herbs and spices, such as Imeretian saffron. This saffron substitute is actually the ground and dried petals of marigold. Along with summer savory, the taste of marigold sets Georgian food apart from that of other cultures using similar spice combinations. Like Indian cooks, Georgians utilize fenugreek, coriander, garlic, chiles, and pepper in their herb and spice mixture of *khmeli-suneli,* but dried marigold and savory replace turmeric. Similarly, cinnamon and vinegar regularly flavor meat in the Georgian diet, just as they do in Arabic cuisines, but marigold rather than true saffron adds the fillip.

The Georgians use spices appropriate to the dish at hand, varying the ingredients and proportions accordingly. Readymade mixtures of *khmeli-suneli* can be bought at the market in hues ranging from pale green to golden to umber, depending on the intended purpose. Many of the best herbs come from Svaneti, the mountainous region bordering Imereti where especially aromatic plants grow on the alpine slopes. For years I hoarded packets of Svanetian *kondari* or summer savory, a local variety of fenugreek *(Trigonella coerulea),* and field mint or *ombalo,* all of which combine to create the flavors so specific to Georgian cuisine.

As for staple foods, Georgians rely on corn and wheat where Persian cooks turn rice to advantage and Armenian cooks use bulghur. Instead of the legumes typically found in the Middle East and Mediterranean—lentils, chick-peas, and favas—Georgians eat a second new-world crop, kidney beans. Walnuts reign over pine nuts and almonds; so much so, in fact, that standard dishes prepared throughout Georgia without nuts, such as the spicy beef soup *kharcho* or the chicken stew *chakhokhbili,* often include nuts in their western Georgian variations. The freshly pressed oil from the walnuts provides the necessary dietary supplement of fat, as do the rich *suluguni* and *imeruli,* fresh-tasting cow's milk cheeses used in place of butter with cornbread.

Within Georgia itself the greatest regional difference between East and West is in the relative degree of spiciness to the food. Eastern Georgians prefer a cool, fresh taste, while western Georgians like to add a zing with fresh and dried hot pepper. A second difference lies in the preference of western Georgians for corn, rather than wheat. Here *mchadi* or corncakes are eaten instead of *puri.* As is evident from their reliance on such ingredients as corn, beans, and peppers, western Georgian cooks have put new-world crops to good use. The tomato is highly appreciated by eastern and western Georgians alike.

*Women sorting grain in the Georgian heartland.*

No matter which part of the country they live in, however, the Georgians remain tied to their land. Even on the eve of the twenty-first century, the most inveterate city dwellers retain a fondness for the rural way of life, escaping to the countryside whenever they can. When it is impossible to leave the city, they visit the market, always an enchanting place. In Tbilisi, the central marketplace has two huge floors of stalls. Mounds of ground spices in earthy hues of red, green, gold, and brown greet the eye, their freshness immediately evident to the nose. Hawkers push their own special blends of *khmeli-suneli* or their farm-cured cheeses and meats, calling out to the shoppers with unabashed hyperbole, vying with each other for poetic expression. A butcher might chide a doubtful customer by crying, "You ask whether this meat is fresh? Are you kidding? Just yesterday it was still grazing in the meadows of Svaneti. Haven't you ever watched the sun rise over the Svanetian hills? Think of those rosy rays illuminating the grazing cattle! Picture them kissed by the morning dew! How can you turn up your nose at the morning dew?"

Leafy bunches of cilantro, opal basil, green basil, tarragon, dill, summer savory, mint, and flat-leafed parsley are laid out in a throne of greens. Purslane, wild garlic, beet greens, and *tsitsmati* supplement the more familiar herbs. And as might be expected for a cuisine featuring a taste for the sour, pickles and marinades infuse the air with their briny odor. In one corner of the market stand barrels with whole heads of garlic soaking in verjuice or pomegranate juice. The heads are peeled to reveal cloves stained a deep purple, which the Georgians pop raw into their mouths. Also displayed are trays of *dzhondzholi* or Colchis bladdernut *(Staphylea colchica)*, an edible ornamental plant with long stems of tightly furled, beadlike tendrils redolent of garlic. Eggplants are sold marinated whole and in pieces, green tomatoes salted or preserved in vinegar.

Fruits also abound. Kartli, the province in which Tbilisi is located, is noted for its orchards, especially its apples and peaches, the best of which come from the environs of Gori, where Stalin was born. I especially love the tiny golden lady apples; the pink gooseberries and red and black currants for pickles and preserves; the many varieties of plums ranging from sour to sweet, purple, yellow, green, and red; the peaches, apricots, pears, and berries; the sweet cherries and sour *shindi* or cornelian cherries, the juice of which Georgian warriors used to drink before battle to fortify their blood.

Beyond the fruits stretch rows of locally grown walnuts, hazelnuts, and almonds, and then heaps of dried fruits, which eventually give way to the cultivated and wild grains, including tiny red kidney beans and various grinds of cornmeal. At the exit, stalls of cut flowers tempt the shopper. Arranged in vases, the flowers envelop even a city apartment in the fragrances of the countryside.

Just as the combinations of ingredients in Georgian dishes are a natural outgrowth of the produce available, so traditional methods of preparation have changed little over the years. Although today's market offers a wider variety of foodstuffs than ever before, Georgians have not been quick to embrace a foreign or fast-food culture. Old recipes and techniques are still proudly passed on from one generation to the next. Because few cookbooks exist, the Ministry of Public Catering recently has undertaken the task of documenting Georgian foodways. But the vast repertory of foods still remains uncharted. To Georgians, eating well is a normal and integral fact of life, one that need not be codified. For this reason, in researching this book I had difficulties in certain households talking my way into the kitchen. My rightful place as a guest belonged at the table, isolated from the labors of cuisine. With persistence, however, I learned that most Georgian foods can be replicated here at home, even if they do lack the resonance of their original setting.

To an extraordinary degree, Georgians integrate the outdoors into their lives, particularly in the spheres of cooking and eating. Whether gathered on a city balcony for a formal meal or by the roadside for an impromptu bite, Georgians consider al fresco dining the best way to eat, a chance to appreciate nature while consuming what it offers. For *sagzali* or picnic foods they'll carry thin, flat loaves of *lavashi* in which to wrap cheese, tomatoes, herbs, or grilled meat. Invariably they will bring some wine, these days transported in bottles rather than in the traditional *tikchora* of sheep or buffalo skin. And rarely do they miss an opportunity to cook over an open flame. Having eaten grilled meat in Georgia, I must agree with Alexandre Dumas when he writes of "the most delicious *shashlyk* [shish-kebab] I have ever tasted." Dumas' meal consisted "not of the usual mutton but of chicken, plover, and partridge, truly a feast." Even this grilled fare seems only a pale reflection of more fabled times, when a proper feast called for a huge ox roasted on a spit, stuffed successively with a calf, a lamb, a turkey, a goose, a duck, and finally a young chicken, seasoned throughout with spices. The culinary art lay in ensuring that each type of meat was perfectly roasted. These days the cook is more likely to offer a choice of beef or lamb, skewered in large chunks. Prepared with fresh meat, this *mtsvadi* is the simplest dish of all: Just impale and enjoy. When meat is older and tougher, however, *basturma* is usually made. *Basturma* is simply meat that has been marinated, usually cut into smaller pieces so that the marinade will penetrate and tenderize. Dumas boasts of having learned to make *basturma* on his Caucasian journey:

Take a joint of mutton—the leg if you can get it—cut it into walnut-sized pieces and leave them to soak for a quarter of an hour in a marinade of onions, vinegar, and liberal amounts of salt and pepper. Meanwhile, prepare a fire.

Impale the pieces of mutton on a wood or metal skewer and rotate the skewer over the coals until the meat is browned. You will find that this is an excellent dish. At least I didn't eat anything better during all of my travels in Russia.

If the morsels of mutton could remain in the marinade overnight or if, when cooked, they could be sprinkled with sumac, they would taste even better. But if you are pressed for time or have no sumac, then it is unnecessary.

Even if you don't have a skewer or happen to be travelling in a place where skewers are unknown, you can always substitute something else. Throughout my travels the cleaning-rod of my carbine served as a skewer, and I didn't notice any harm to the worthiness of my weapon from using it in this humble role.

—from *Le Caucase* (1859)

Grilling is still a favorite way of preparing foods (which is not surprising if we recall that Georgia was the legendary place where Prometheus gave fire to mankind). Although the ancients considered grilling the most primitive of cooking methods, and boiling the most refined, grilling has always suited the Georgians. It is convenient for the impromptu picnics they love. Georgians frequently cook not only meats and vegetables but also breads and stews over an open flame.

A second standard method of preparing food is by slow cooking, and Georgian cuisine has an extensive repertoire of soups and stews. Hearty stews are particularly well appreciated in the mountain regions as fortification against the elements. Prudent cooks often take advantage of the heat remaining in the *toné* after breadbaking to prepare a roast such as *purnis mtsvadi,* lamb cooked slowly in a clay pot.

While few of us have access to a clay oven, not much equipment is necessary to prepare the remaining Georgian foods. Perhaps the single most important implement in the traditional Georgian kitchen is a mortar and pestle for grinding nuts and spices. (For ease of preparation in the American kitchen, it is perfectly acceptable to substitute a food processor for the nuts and a coffee grinder for the spices.) In addition to a variety of stockpots and pans, earthenware casseroles make authentic containers for slow-cooked stews. It is also helpful to have a heavy cast-iron skillet for making fried chicken and corncakes.

Western Georgians cook both of these specialties in *ketsi* ranging in diameter from six to twelve inches. The use of the *ketsi* is an example of how the Georgians have continued the practice of ancient cooking methods. Earthenware pots were known to the Egyptians, who used them to bake over an open fire. By stacking the pots one atop the other, they sealed in moisture, creating an oven, in effect. Today, in urban apartments, the foods traditionally prepared in *ketsis* can successfully be made indoors on the cooktop. If you are cooking outdoors, however, it is useful to have a grill and sturdy skewers that can accommodate large pieces of meat.

Following are some of the ingredients typically used to prepare Georgian foods. I have included their Georgian names in case you should find yourself at the Tbilisi market. Many of the ingredients are seasonal for those of us who live in cool climates, but even in my small New England town I have found a produce store willing to supply fresh herbs throughout the year. Because some Georgian recipes rely for both taste and texture on vast quantities of herbs, it is inadvisable to substitute the dried variety. So, if you find yourself unable to secure a source for fresh greens, it is best to postpone trying that recipe until summertime. Opt instead for a recipe that demands only a handful of herbs for garnish—a decidedly Georgian touch, but one that is not essential to the overall success of the dish.

## F R E S H    H E R B S

✳ BASIL *(rekhani) [ocimum basilicum; ocimum basilicum purpurascens, var. "dark opal"]*. Georgians enjoy two different kinds of basil, the sweet green-leafed plant most familiar to Americans and the purple-leafed dark opal basil. Sweet basil originated in India and was imported to Georgia by traveling merchants. Ironically, the aromatic spiciness of dark opal basil seems more purely Georgian in taste, even though, as it happens, this cultivar was only recently developed in the United States. When serving a platter of fresh greens, it is nice to present both varieties.

✳ CELERY *(niakhuri) [Apium graveolens]*. Georgians rarely eat the stalks of celery. They buy this vegetable mainly for the leaves, which they use to flavor stews. Finding leafy stalks can be a problem for American shoppers, since supermarket celery is usually sold prepackaged with most of the leaves removed. I sometimes resort to buying several packages of celery stalks, then cut off enough leaves for my purposes.

✳ CILANTRO *(kindzi) [Coriandrum sativum]*. Cilantro, also known as fresh coriander or Chinese parsley, is the most essential herb in Georgian cooking. Some Americans find the slightly metallic flavor of this herb to be an acquired taste, but it adds a surprising depth and excitement to Georgian foods, both as a garnish and as an integral ingredient. Georgians like cilantro so much that they eat it out of hand. Cilantro is sometimes hard to find year-round in the stores, though Chinese and Hispanic markets usually carry it. The herb is also easy to grow from seed, and a few plants in pots on the windowsill can carry you through the winter. Remove any tough stalks before chopping and measuring.

✳ DILL *(kama) [Anethum graveolens]*. Georgians use the feathery leaves of this herb to season meats and vegetables. Dried dillweed is one of the components of the flavoring mixture *khmeli-suneli*. Discard any tough stems before chopping.

✳ FENNEL *(tseretso) [Foeniculum vulgare]*. The ripe fronds of the fennel plant are often used to flavor the Georgian plum sauce, *tkemali*, or alternatively, the seeds are dried and ground.

✳ MINT *(pitna) [Mentha piperita]*. Mint grows wild throughout much of Georgia, and like other herbs it is used in copious amounts. In western Georgia the favored mint is *ombalo (mentha pulegium)*, a rather delicate plant that grows as freely as dandelions do here. I recommend peppermint for the recipes in this book.

✳ PARSLEY *(okhrakhushi) [Petroselinum crispum, sativum]*. Georgians use the flat-leafed Italian parsley rather than the curly variety more common here. As with cilantro and dill, remove any tough stalks before using.

✳ SUMMER SAVORY *(kondari) [Satureja hortensis L.]*. Like other herbs, summery savory is used both fresh and dried to flavor meats, vegetables, and stews. While it is virtually impossible to find fresh summer savory at the grocery, this herb is readily available from specialized nurseries and is remarkably easy to grow. Use both the leaves and the fine stems of the plant.

✳ TARRAGON *(tarkhuna) [Artemisia dracunculus]*. Georgians like tarragon so much that they even drink an emerald-green tarragon-flavored soda. Fresh tarragon adds character to meat stews and cheese dishes. It is not generally used dried.

# DRIED HERBS AND SPICES

✳ BARBERRY *(kotsakhuri) [Berberis vulgaris]*. The barberry is the small, sour fruit of a thorny shrub. Georgians use it dried and ground. They also cook the berries down into *kvatsarakhi,* a thick, extremely sour syrup used to flavor stews. Ground sumac *(Rhus coriaria),* readily available at Middle Eastern food stores, may be substituted for dried barberry.

✳ BAY LEAF *(dapna) [Lauris nobilis]*. Bay laurel trees thrive in western Georgia, particularly on the Black Sea coast. As they do along the coastal range in California, Georgian cooks use the leaves fresh to infuse meat and vegetable dishes with their rich oil. Dried leaves are an acceptable substitute.

✳ CARAWAY *(kvliavi) [Carum carvi]*. Caraway, a favorite ingredient in dishes from the Georgian highlands, is used ground. Buy the seeds and grind them in a coffee mill or spice grinder.

✳ CINNAMON *(darichini) [Cinnamomum zeylanicum Br.]*. Try to find true cinnamon rather than cassia, which often parades as cinnamon in the United States. Georgians use this spice ground.

✳ CLOVES *(mikhaki) [Eugenia caryophyllus]*. Cloves are used ground much as cinnamon is, to flavor soups and stews.

✳ CORIANDER *(kindzi) [Coriandrum sativum]*. The ground seeds of the coriander plant flavor a wide range of foods, from meats to vegetables to breads. Coriander provides a quintessentially Georgian taste. For the best flavor, buy whole seeds and grind them yourself.

✳ FENUGREEK *(utskho suneli) [Trigonella coerulea]*. Dried and ground, fenugreek is an important component of the herb and spice mixture *khmeli-suneli,* and often a pinch is added independently to soups and stews. The Georgian name for fenugreek means "foreign aromatic"; most likely the spice was introduced from India. Dried fenugreek leaves can be bought in Indian food stores; grind them to a powder before using.

✳ KHMELI-SUNELI. This mixture typically contains ground dried coriander seed, ground celery seed, dried basil, dill, parsley, fenugreek, summer savory, bay leaf, and mint. Ground dried marigold petals are often added as well. A basic recipe for *khmeli-suneli* appears on page 184. However, since the proportions of ingredients vary depending on the basis of each dish, the recipes in this book call for individual spices rather than for a specific mixture of *khmeli-suneli.*

✳ MARIGOLD *(imeruli shaphrani)* *[Tagetes patula; Calendula officin-alis]*. The Georgians use marigold frequently, referring to it as "Imere-tian saffron" after the western Georgian province of Imereti where the dried petals of the plant are most appreciated. Marigold was exten-sively cultivated in the Middle Ages, and in his famous seventeenth-century herbal Nicholas Culpeper called it "a herb of the sun." Geor-gians continue to use marigold today, but unlike others who also use it for culinary purposes (the French and the Dutch in particular), Georgians prefer the dried and ground petals of the *tagetes* marigold to the calendula plant. The flavor of marigold is particularly compati-ble with cinnamon and cloves. There is no real substitute for it. If unavailable, marigold can be omitted from the recipes in this book, although the final product will lack a certain earthy flavor. Since mari-golds are easy to grow in the garden or in pots, it makes sense to dry the petals yourself and then grind them into a fine powder. Dried marigold may also be ordered by mail from Aphrodisia, 282 Bleecker Street, New York, NY 10014; (212) 989-6440.

✳ PEPPER *(pilpili, tsitsaka)* *[Piper nigrum; Capsicum annum]*. Geor-gians use black pepper *(pilpili)* liberally. Western Georgians are also very fond of chile peppers *(tsitsaka)*, both dried and fresh. Tbilisi's Food Industry Research Institute has devoted considerable attention to the analysis of hot red pepper. Their studies show that normal intake is .008 grams a day, but in western Georgia, in the province of Samegrelo, up to 2 grams a day are consumed. Thoughtfully enough, Food Institute dieticians are concerned about the Samegrelian diet and have launched a campaign to educate western Georgians about the potential perils of pepper (too much pepper can cause ulcers).

Many of my recipes call for both cayenne and paprika to approxi-mate the flavor of the dried hot chile pepper used in Georgia. When fresh hot peppers are called for, use the small varieties such as red or green jalapeños or serranos.

## OTHER INGREDIENTS

✳ ADZHIKA. The favorite Georgian condiment made from fresh hot chile peppers, *adzhika* ranges in consistency from a thick paste to a liquid relish like salsa. It is a classic accompaniment to grilled meats. If necessary, substitute a very hot salsa. A milder green *adzhika* may also be prepared from herbs. See page 181 for a recipe.

✳ BREAD *(puri)*. Even Georgia's largest cities boast old-fashioned bakeries where *kartuli puri* or Georgian bread is baked in the traditional *toné*. It's easy to stop by a commercial bakery and pick up several loaves of bread still hot from the ovens. And, as a bonus, you can watch the breadmaking in progress. Because *puri* grows stale quickly, it must be baked daily. Its ingenious shape is designed to please all consumers: An elongated oval, the loaf is thicker in the center than at the edges, so that lovers of both crust and chewy interior can enjoy their favorite textures.

Stoking and baking in the *toné* are laborious processes. First, a starter prepared from yeast, flour, water, and salt is poured into a special dough trough or *vartsli,* with just enough flour mixed in to make a soft dough. The amount of salt in the dough is crucial. Too much, and the taste is unpleasant. Too little, and the bread won't stick to the sides of the oven, resulting in a *kuti puri* or "crippled bread," burned and covered with ashes.

A very hot fire is made from dried grapevines on the floor of the *toné,* and soon flames come roaring out of the top like a B-movie volcano. By the time the flames die down, the sides of the oven have been coated with black ashes, which soon turn white, indicating that the oven has reached proper temperature. While the oven is heating, the baker presses the dough into 10-inch ovals, being careful to avoid uniform thickness.

*Rural women baking bread in a* toné.

Salted water is then splashed against the sides of the oven to test the temperature. When the water instantly sizzles, a metal lid is placed over the burning vines, then some old ashes are scooped up and water added to them to make a rather dry mix which is sprinkled over the lid to cool down the fire. The baker next runs a piece of wet burlap along the sides of the *toné* to clean it of ashes. Now, working quickly, he or she picks up an oval of dough, splashes it lightly with salted water, then slaps it directly onto the side of the oven.

The first loaves, the thin round *lavashi,* are placed low in the oven, closer to the source of heat. My favorite *shoti,* or batons, are placed against the top rim of the *toné,* creating a lovely pattern. The bread bakes on one side only, and within eight minutes, the first batch is done. Each loaf is pierced with a hook to secure it, then a spatula is used to remove it from the wall of the oven. (The very first loaf, the *dedis kveri* or "mother" loaf, is considered a special treat for children.) Whenever space is freed, new loaves are slapped on. Each round takes progressively longer to bake as the oven loses its heat, until a new stoking is required.

Other breads are differentiated mainly by their shape. A common daily loaf is the round *madaduri,* with approximately one-third of its surface thin and crusty, the remainder thick and chewy. The *kutkhiani* is a flat, rectangular loaf, while the *trakhtinuli* is a flat oval. At Easter-time *basila* is prepared, a leavenless bread similar to matzoh. Unlike the other Georgian breads, *basila* is baked in a *ketsi* rather than in the *toné.* A cross or sun is inscribed into the middle of each round sheet of bread. In Kartli province, religious practice called for the water from an infant's baptism to be sprinkled on the *toné* to sanctify the bread.

Because the intense heat and smoke from the *toné* lend Georgian bread a distinctive taste, it cannot easily be reproduced in a standard oven. To serve bread with a Georgian meal, the best alternative to building your own *toné* is to buy a crusty peasant-style loaf from a good bakery.

✳ BUTTER *(karaki).* Unless otherwise specified, use salted butter for the recipes in this book. Historically, the best butter comes from the mountainous region of Khevsureti, where the local people once used it as currency. Butter churned in May was especially prized for its vivid color, as yellow as the yolks of eggs. Throughout the summer, as the alpine meadow grasses matured, the butter grew progressively paler in color.

Some older recipes stipulate *erbo* or clarified butter—a result of Indian culinary influence—but I find this unnecessary to the success of the dish. Also unnecessary is the use of fat from the fat-tailed sheep, called for in many traditional recipes. This fat adds a gutsy flavor to meat dishes, but is too strong for most American palates.

❋ CHEESE *(khveli)*. Georgians eat abundant cheese, and each region has its own specialty. Mountain people prefer sharp, briny sheep's cheese such as *gudis khveli* or *tushuri*, which is aged in sheepskin (the stomach) until quite pungent. Most mountain cheeses are made by maturing the curds in skins rather than pitchers or vats, and the art of the cheesemaker is considered akin to that of the vintner. For one traditional type of *tushuri*, a hole is dug in the ground and lined with the leaves of wild sorrel. The curds are poured into a bag, which is placed in the hole as a protection against the harsh elements. When the cheese begins to ferment, it is transferred to a *guda* or sheepskin for further aging. Toward the end of the nineteenth century, *tushuri* cheese was in such demand that twenty thousand pounds of it were imported annually into Tbilisi.

Elsewhere in Georgia, milder cow's milk cheeses are preferred. *Chechi* or string cheese is popular, as is *suluguni,* the most widely used Georgian cheese. *Suluguni* is usually sold in large rounds up to a foot in diameter, but for special occasions it is prepared in flat, individual disks, which can be thinly rolled. Cheese is the essential ingredient for the famous Georgian bread *khachapuri*. Mozzarella makes an adequate substitute for *suluguni*.

❋ CORNELIAN CHERRY *(shindi) [Cornus mas]*. Georgians dry these bright red fruits of a flowering shrub and use them to lend a pleasant tartness to meat and vegetable dishes. They are the featured ingredient in *zetis kupatebi*, dumplings stuffed with cornelian cherries and onions, then fried in walnut oil. Cornelian cherries also make an excellent jam. I have found a good substitute to be the tart dried cherries available by mail order from American Spoon Foods, Inc., 411 East Lake Street, Petoskey, MI 49770; or from Chukar Cherry Company, 306 Wine Country Road, P.O. Box 510, Prosser, WA 99350.

❋ CORNMEAL *(gomi)*. *Gomi* is an ancient millet *(setaria italica [L.]P.B.)*, which was once grown extensively in Georgia. After corn was introduced from Turkey in the sixteenth century, the cultivation of the original *gomi* was gradually abandoned. By the late eighteenth century, corn was widespread in western Georgia, and by the end of the nineteenth century it prevailed as the more reliable and palatable crop. The name *gomi* is still used, however, to refer to cornmeal and grits, as well as to the cooked porridge made from them. *Gomi* is eaten primarily in western Georgia. For the most authentic taste and best texture, use stone-ground white grits. An excellent source is Kenston Kitchens, P.O. Box 88215, Atlanta, GA 30356-8215.

✳ EGGPLANT *(badridzhani)*. The Georgians use small eggplants, those we call Japanese, rather than the large globes commonly found in our markets. The recipes in this book have been tested with both varieties and will work well as long as the eggplant is not bitter. If in doubt, salt the eggplant after slicing and allow the bitter juices to drain before cooking.

✳ FEIJOA *(pheihoa)* *[Feijoa sellowiana]*. This pale green, aromatic fruit grows on the Black Sea coast. Its flavor is reminiscent of pineapples and guavas. California produces a small crop of fabulous feijoas. They are available by mail from Cravings, P.O. Box 4430, Portland, OR 97208. For feijoa relish, see page 185.

✳ GARLIC *(niori)*. Fresh garlic is an absolute necessity in Georgian cuisine, which makes use of both the bulbs and tender shoots. Avoid dried garlic powder or flakes. The most intense flavor is concentrated in small, compact heads of garlic, rather than in large heads of elephant garlic.

✳ GRAPES *(qurdzeni)*. In a country where grapes provide much of the livelihood and are so revered, it is not surprising that no part of the plant is wasted. If the grape skins are not added to the pressed juice for Kakhetian-style wine, they are used to make Georgian *chacha* or vodka. *Isrimi* or verjuice (the freshly pressed juice of unripe grapes) is used in cooking to lend a tart, sour taste to soups and stews. Boiled until thick and concentrated, the fresh juice becomes *badagi,* the basis for healthful desserts. Some grapes are dried into raisins. The leaves are used fresh or preserved for *tolma*s. And even the dried vines are fashioned into skewers.

✳ HONEY *(tapli)*. Georgia is known for its excellent honey. At the market it is sold in several forms—as a regular viscous syrup; dry and pressed into a block; and still dripping in the comb. Any floral honey will work well for the recipes in this book, but avoid strong-tasting honeys such as buckwheat.

✳ NUTS *(kakali)*. Walnuts *(nigozi)* are the most widely used nut in Georgian cuisine, although Georgians also enjoy hazelnuts *(tkhili)*.

Almonds are used less frequently. A very sweet and exotic jam is made from unripe green walnuts that have been treated with slaked lime and alum. Flavored with cardamom and cloves, this jam is a seasonal specialty. Ripe walnuts should be fresh and oily. If they lack aroma, heat them briefly in a dry cast-iron skillet to release their flavor. Georgia's most famous sauce is *satsivi,* the main component of which is walnuts. The nuts are ground, then pounded exactingly by hand to a fine paste. In Georgia this pounding is carried out with mortar and pestle until the nuts release a golden oil, prized as a garnish. Once the oil has been drawn off, spices and herbs are added to the nuts, and the mixture is pounded further until it becomes a thick paste. Finally the nuts are forced through a fine sieve to remove any lumps. In the West, this task can be facilitated by the food processor.

Although Georgian purists would claim that simple grinding by machine is insufficient to release the best flavor of the nuts, I have opted for convenience. Despite the nontraditional method, the recipes here will turn out well as long as the nuts are sufficiently ground. When a recipe calls for finely ground nuts, grind them just to the point when a paste is about to form. If too finely ground, the paste will not incorporate well into other ingredients. If not finely enough ground, the nuts will not bind properly.

✳ OIL *(zeti). Zeti* is another borrowed culinary term, this time from the Semitic. Olive oil was the oil of preference for many centuries, so much so that the Georgians know olives as *zetiskhili* or "oil fruit." The Georgian repertory does not contain the series of special "olive-oil dishes" so integral to neighboring Turkish cuisine. Instead, walnuts were regularly pressed for their rich oil, and once corn became an established crop, corn oil was frequently used. Today, the most readily available oil is sunflower oil, although this reflects Soviet agricultural practices more than Georgian taste. Unless otherwise specified, I have used corn oil for the recipes in this book. For recipes requiring a small amount of walnut oil, the oil may be purchased, imported from France, at any well-stocked specialty food store.

✳ POMEGRANATES *(brotseuli).* Pomegranates are prized in Georgian cuisine both for their ruby seeds and for their juice, which is used fresh and as the base for *masharabi,* a flavoring syrup for stews. To make *masharabi,* the fresh pomegranate juice is cooked with cinnamon, cloves, and just a bit of sugar until thick; it is meant to remain sour. Although the season for fresh pomegranates is short, the seeds may be scraped out and frozen for year-round use. Bottled pomegranate juice, available at health-food stores, may be used in place of fresh juice or *masharabi*.

✳ TKEMALI *[Prunus divaricata]*. *Tkemali* is a sour plum that grows throughout Georgia. The word also refers to the piquant sauce made from this plum, which is used as both a seasoning in soups, stews, and vegetable dishes and as a condiment for grilled meats. *Tkemali* sauce is piquant, hot, and slightly sweet at the same time. It is served fresh or preserved for winter keeping. Because the *tkemali* plum is unavailable here, I substitute Santa Rosa plums, preferring them to be slightly underripe. A recipe for *tkemali* sauce appears on page 119.

✳ TKLAPI. *Tklapi* is dried fruit leather, made by boiling *tkemali* or sour plums, then puréeing them and spreading the purée into a sheet to dry. This fruit leather is an incomparable souring agent for soups and stews, less astringent than vinegar, more flavorful than tomatoes. The Georgians add no sulphur as a preservative, so their homemade *tklapi* is a dark reddish brown. Fruit leather is also made from sweeter fruits like apricots and peaches, in which case it is intended for eating out of hand rather than cooking. I have found that the commercially produced fruit leather available here works well in recipes calling for *tklapi*, even though it is somewhat sweet. Fruit leather may be purchased at Middle Eastern or health-food stores; camping-supply stores often carry it, too. Instructions for homemade *tklapi* are on page 188.

✳ VINEGAR *(dzmari)*. I generally use red wine vinegar for the recipes in this book, but white wine vinegar and cider vinegar are perfectly acceptable if a more delicate or fruitier taste is desired.

✳ YOGURT *(matsoni)*. Georgian yogurt is some of the best in the world, whether made from cow's milk or the even richer water buffalo milk. *Matsoni* is never gelatinous but always shimmery, with a pleasant tartness. It is eaten alone for breakfast or added to soups, vegetable dishes, and stews. When using store-bought yogurt, avoid the nonfat variety, which lacks body.

# WINE

If food is the heart of the Georgian feast, then its spirit resides in wine *(ghvino)*, and no discussion of Georgian cuisine would be complete without mentioning this drink. The center of wine growing in Georgia is Kakheti, located in the eastern portion of the country. Here the annual autumn *rtveli* or wine harvest is still celebrated with songs dating back to ancient times, their rhythms meant to accompany the various stages of processing, from the trimming of the vines to the pressing of the grapes.

Kakheti is known for its unique method of wine making, which differs considerably from standard European practices. After the grapes are pressed, the juice is fermented together with the skins, stems, and seeds of the plant to yield a taste specific to the wines of this region—raisiny with a hint of Madeira—and with a lovely, deep amber hue. Georgian researchers, ever eager to point out the nutritional benefits of their cuisine, have frequently turned their attention to the native wines. They tout a sort of wine therapy based on the moderate consumption of homemade wine, which when prepared by the Kakhetian method preserves vitamins otherwise lost with the discarded skins. Stories abound of old people cured of the aftereffects of stroke by regularly eating bread dipped in wine. Indeed, Kakhetian wines do contain a high proportion of Vitamin P, which increases the elasticity of the blood and thus serves as a good preventive against hypertension. As for the diet of bread and wine, it is a long-standing tradition. One of Georgia's most ancient dishes, at one time served only to kings, is *boglitso,* boiled wine into which bread is dipped. This practice probably derived from the Greeks, who regularly breakfasted on bread and undiluted wine.

Because the Kakhetian method is so labor-intensive, it is dying out as a commercial process, and most modern vintners now produce wine by the European method. Consequently, the only true Kakhetian wines you're likely to taste have been prepared at home. But whether commercially or domestically produced, the single most important piece of wine-making equipment remains the *kvevri,* a large, red clay amphora. The best *kvevri*s come from the firm of Labadze in the village of Shrosha, where the factory yard is a wonderland of vessels: side-by-side with miniature souvenir *kvevri*s holding little more than a single swallow of liquid lie genuine *kvevri*s, towering six feet and more into the air, for the serious storage of wine. The relationship of the *kvevri* to wine is similar to that of the *toné* to bread: While it is possible to make both of these basic products without using clay implements, the taste the clay affords is incomparable.

Nearly every Georgian country household has a *marani,* a place for burying the *kvevri*s up to their necks in the earth, where the temperature remains cool and steady. If the house lacks a cellar with an earthen floor, the *kvevri* are dug right into the ground outdoors. One of the largest *marani*s in Georgia is at Tsinandali, the restored nine-teenth-century home of Prince Alexander Chavchavadze, a Romantic poet. Chavchavadze frequently entertained foreigners at his estate, in-cluding many of the exiled Russian Decembrists. Familiar with Euro-pean ways, Chavchavadze built Georgia's first large winery, and the highly regarded dry white Tsinandali wine is still produced there by the European method. In Chavchavadze's *marani* the visitor can see a traditional wine press or *satsnakheli*, a huge trough made of walnut or stone into which workers climbed to press the grapes with their feet. The *marani* also displays an enormous *kvevri* with a capacity of 3,500 liters, or nearly 1,000 gallons. In comparison, most household *kvevri*s are designed to hold 300 liters, or about 70 gallons.

In making wine by the Kakhetian method, the pressed grape juice, skins, stems, and seeds are poured into the buried *kvevri*s and stirred four or six times a day for three to five months. This new wine is known as *machari*. When the wine has reached the right degree of fermentation, it is drawn off from the lees. If produced commercially, the wine is transferred to oak barrels to age for at least a year, but homemade wine is usually ladled by means of a special long-handled gourd *(khrika)* from the first *kvevri* into even smaller *kvevri*s for the aging process. These *kvevri*s are topped with a wooden lid, then sealed with mud. Since it is imperative to keep air out of the *kvevri* lest it spoil the wine, dirt is mounded all over and around the lid; stepping into a *marani* is like visiting the burrows of gophers, each of which has left its trace on the earth. Whenever wine is taken off in any quantity, the remainder is transferred to progressively smaller vessels.

The *kvevri* resonates with the accumulation of centuries of culture and celebration. When a boy is born, a *kvevri* of new wine is often sunk into the ground and opened only on the boy's wedding day. Once empty and overturned, the *kvevri* symbolizes abundance. Even the art of using the *kvevri* has given rise to much lore. Georgians joke about the largest of these vessels, and one popular film spoofs the dangers of climbing into a *kvevri* for cleaning. In the film, a prosper-ous, rotund vintner gets trapped inside the massive *kvevri* he has pur-chased at considerable expense, and predictably, the *kvevri* begins to roll downhill, gathering speed and eventually smashing, leaving the vintner nettled and dazed. In fact, real skill is required to clean these vessels, and only a person of minimum girth can last in this business. The cleaner climbs down a ladder through the narrow neck into the dark interior of the *kvevri*. Using a special implement constructed of pieces of cherry bark layered together about six inches thick, then pierced with a long stick for a handle, he scrubs the bottom and sides with water. After washing the *kvevri,* the cleaner places a cloth over the bark and wipes the remaining water dry.

Whereas a *marani* is a poetic place, dark and heavy with the ripe smell of grapes, Kakheti's huge Kindzmarauli wine-storage facility more closely resembles a James Bond set. Here all is technology, without a single *kvevri* in sight. Stainless-steel holding tanks with voluminous pipes stretch for nearly five miles through a series of tunnels cut into the depths of a mountainside, where the temperature remains constant. The main tunnel, wide enough for vehicles to pass, runs for almost a mile, with tributary tunnels branching off it. The Sunday we managed to talk our way into the facility, it was dark and deserted, the only illumination provided by the headlights of our car, which lit up endless cells of vats behind impenetrable gratings. We felt nervous, half expecting armed security guards to materialize out of the darkness and challenge our presence. Our visit proved uneventful, however—a cool respite from the ninety-degree heat outside.

Visitors throughout the ages have commented on the excellence and lavishness of Georgian wines; they are also inclined to tell tall tales of Georgian drinking habits. Two of the most articulate travelers to Georgia, Sir John Chardin and Alexandre Dumas, left accounts of their drinking travails in this land. Their tales seem surprising for Frenchmen, whom we tend to think of as able drinkers in their own right. Though Chardin praises the excellence of the local wine, he claims that at one feast he attended, four men "from Ten in the Morning till Ten in the Evening . . . Drank out a whole Charge of Wine, that weigh'd Three Hundred Pound Weight."

Difficult as it may be to gauge the extent of Chardin's exaggeration, what can be verified is the importance Georgians ascribe to the ritual of drinking, the way in which they honor the fruit of the vine. For instance, it is not acceptable to pour with the left hand, nor should one ever pour wine away from the body rather than toward it. American casualness and informality can seem disrespectful to those who believe in handling wine with reverence.

Georgians usually drink wine from glass or crystal goblets, but on special occasions the *tamada* will call for a more traditional drinking vessel, usually a *kantsi* or wine horn. These horns come in a range of sizes, the largest holding a liter or more to test the drinker's ability: Unless the horn is empty, it is impossible to set it down without spilling the contents. Over the centuries Georgians developed a number of specialized vessels for serving and drinking wine, perfecting ritual to an art. Chardin was struck by the variety of containers he saw at a royal wedding in Tbilisi:

> But that which was most to be wonder'd at after all this excellent order, was the Court Cupboard which contain'd about a Hundred and Twenty Vessels, that appertain'd to Drinking, Bowls, Cups, Horns, Sixty Flagons and Twelve Jugs. The Jugs were for the most part Silver. The Bowls and Cups were some of Polish'd Gold, others Gold Enamell'd, some set with pretious Stones, others only Silver; the Horns were Embellish'd after the same manner as the Richer sort of Cups; and of several proportions. The ordinary ones were about Eight Inches High, Broad at the Top about Two, very black and Polish'd. Some were of Rhinoceros's Snouts, others of Dears Horns, whereas the Common sort were made of the Horns of Oxen and Sheep.
>
> —*The Travels of Sir John Chardin into Persia and the East-Indies . . .* (1686)

Traditional Georgian families still use special vessels to bring wine to table, such as the *chapi,* a two-handled jug with a squat neck and bulbous body tapering to a narrow base. From the transitional vessel the wine is poured into a variety of other containers, meant either for pouring at table or drinking. Quite common are the *khelada,* a single-handled pitcher (from the Georgian word *kheli* or "hand"), and the more elaborate *deda-khelada* or "mother jug," composed of a central pitcher with several smaller pitchers affixed to the sides, like a mother with numerous breasts. On festive occasions the *marani* is used, a decorative jug fashioned in the shape of an animal, often a ram or stag. The spout of the *marani,* from which the wine is drunk, forms the head of the animal, suggesting connections with the pagan world of antiquity.

*Hammered silver wine ewers.*

Other drinking vessels include shallow, bowl-like goblets, variously known as *tasi, dzhami,* or *azarpesh,* depending on their specific shapes. When I invite guests for a Georgian meal, I like to bring out the *kula* friends gave me, an ornately carved piece of wood like a gourd, decorated with metal filigree. The *kula* has only one small opening, at the end of a long handle that also serves as the drinking spout. Like the horn, the *kula* cannot be set down unless emptied.

Following is a description of some of the most readily available Georgian wines, though these commercial products do not compare to the best homemade wines that most families prefer to drink. (Too often one bottle is not as good as the next, as the wineries suffer from problems with quality control.) The wines are generally named after the district where they are produced.

### Red Wines

*Khvanchkara.* Khvanchkara is a semisweet wine made from the Alexandrouli and Mudzhuretuli varietals cultivated on the southern slope of the Rioni River gorge in western Georgia. This wine has a raspberry flavor and dark ruby color. It is much favored by Georgians.

*Kindzmarauli.* Reputedly Stalin's favorite, Kindzmarauli is heavy and blood red, with a lingering sweetness. It is made from Saperavi grapes in the Kakheti district of Kindzmarauli.

*Muzukani.* Mukuzani is made in Kakheti from Saperavi grapes. Rather tannic, Mukuzani is considered therapeutic. It ages better than many Georgian wines. Produced since 1892, it is one of the older commercial varieties.

*Saperavi.* Produced in Kakheti from Saperavi grapes, this wine is full-bodied, with a dark pomegranate color.

*Teliani.* As both substance and subject, Teliani is the favored wine of Russian literati. This is a full-bodied wine, with a dark ruby color, made since 1893 primarily from Cabernet grapes.

## White Wines

*Gurdzhaani.* Gurdzhaani is made by the European method from Rkatsiteli and Mtsvane grapes. (Rkatsiteli is the most widely cultivated varietal in Georgia.) It is slightly bitter in taste and pale golden in color. Gurdzhaani has been commercially produced only since 1943.

*Lykhny.* Lykhny is a rosé wine produced from the Izabella varietal in Abkhazia on the Black Sea coast. It is much sought after in Georgia and Russia as one of the few commercial rosé wines available.

*Napareuli.* Napareuli is made from Rkatsiteli and Mtsvane grapes grown on the left bank of the Alazani River, near the famous brandy producing towns of Gremi and Eniseli. The mild climate of this region lends a characteristic delicate taste to this wine, which is less robust than most Georgian wines.

*Sviri.* Sviri is one of the few commercial wines produced in western Georgia by the Imeretian method, in which the clarified must is repeatedly supplemented with newly pressed juice. After fermentation, the wine is twice drawn off into smaller containers, resulting in a beverage of beautiful amber hue. Sviri is made from the local varietals of Tsolikouri, Tsitska, and Krakhuna grapes.

*Tetra.* Tetra is semisweet and fruity. It is made from Rachuli-Tetra grapes cultivated in the Rioni River gorge.

*Tibaani.* Tibaani is made by the Kakhetian method from Rkatsiteli and Mtsvane grapes. Amber in color, raisiny in flavor, this full-bodied wine is particularly enjoyed by Georgians.

*Tsinandali.* The most popular commercially produced white wine in Georgia, Tsinandali is produced from Rkatsiteli and Mtsvane grapes at Chavchavadze's famous cellars. It is pale straw-colored and fruity.

PART II

# RECIPES AND MENUS

# A NOTE ON
# THE RECIPES

**G**eorgian cooking practices are freehanded, relying on experience rather than on written recipes. There exists no Georgian *Fanny Farmer* or *Joy of Cooking,* in which recipes are standardized and procedures explained. Yet as a nation, Georgia is passionate about food, and many Georgians seem to have a gift for seasoning. An understanding of the basic ingredients that are used in Georgian food allows cooks to experiment while still remaining within the scope of traditional cuisine.

I have arranged the recipes in the conventional categories found in most American cookbooks, although some foods straddle two categories. For instance, appetizers are not passed around as finger foods in Georgia, nor are they eaten singly as a first course. Instead, they are displayed abundantly on the table at the beginning of the meal and may be nibbled throughout. Therefore, under the category of appetizers I have simply listed appropriate foods for which the recipes are given elsewhere in the book. Feel free to mix dishes from several different chapters to make a Georgian-style feast. For an American-style meal, many of these foods, such as turkey *satsivi* or beef patties, can stand on their own as entrées.

Browsing through the recipes, the reader should not be alarmed that many involve the same ingredients. All dishes made with walnuts and cilantro do not taste alike! Much depends on the method of preparation; even when the basic ingredients vary only slightly, Georgian foods offer a surprising variety in taste. I urge you to try them all.

I also encourage you to be flexible with seasonings. If you like your food spicy, by all means add more hot red pepper. If you're a fancier of garlic, then feel free to increase the number of cloves. Georgian food is highly adaptable to this sort of tinkering. The only strict rule governing ingredients involves the amount of nuts in a recipe, which is carefully calculated in balance with a souring agent to yield a dish that is pleasingly rich yet tart. Use a free hand with herbs; increase the proportion of nuts at your own risk.

Because of the inherent flexibility of most of these recipes, I have opted not to specify volume measures for such ingredients as garlic, onions, and green peppers. I give numbers instead. "Two onions, finely chopped" is more in the spirit of Georgian cooking than "two cups finely chopped onion," since most Georgians cook by eye rather than measure. Again, much depends on personal taste. Unless otherwise noted, I used large cloves of garlic when testing these recipes, simply because I like garlic, but the dishes would be equally successful with a less pronounced garlic taste. If I was left with an extra handful of herbs after chopping, I usually threw them into the pot for good measure. Like all Georgian cooks I know, I believe in the spirit of lagniappe, the extra pinch that adds a fillip and bespeaks a generous nature.

# APPETIZERS

**T**he following recipes are all excellent starters for a Georgian meal. When planning which dishes to set out, keep in mind that flavors should be complementary. A cool pickle, for instance, provides a refreshing counterpoint to a piquant purée of vegetables. Sauced dishes combine well with bread, which easily conveys to the mouth any juices still lingering on the plate. Try to choose contrasting colors and textures to stimulate the diners' palates and to make the table festive.

Carousal in a Vine Pergola

# SOUPS

**G**eorgians love soup and are likely to transform almost any ingredient on hand into a satisfying broth. Some of the most traditional soups are the most effortless to prepare, such as a thick *kharcho* made from stale bread moistened with yogurt, or an old-fashioned *shechamandi* of nothing more than water, flour, and a copious amount of pounded garlic. The soups I offer here are, for the most part, more complex in their flavors. Following is a selection of some of my favorite soups, both hearty and light, to accompany the changing seasons.

## BEEF SOUP WITH HERBS
### (Kharcho)

*Kharcho* is a redolent soup as thick as a light stew. Its name is almost generic, referring to beef, lamb, chicken, or even vegetable stocks. But common to all *kharcho*s are a special mixture of *khmeli-suneli,* a liberal dose of herbs, and a souring agent such as a fruit leather, *tkemali* sauce, or vinegar. *Kharcho* is so popular in Georgia that some soup kitchens devote themselves entirely to its preparation.

My favorite *kharcho,* lively with the taste of fresh herbs, is made from beef. Though it tastes best served the same day it is made, this soup may also be prepared in advance, with the herbs added at the last minute.

SERVES 8 TO 10

2 pounds lean stewing beef, cut into ¾-inch cubes
1 pound veal or beef bones
2 quarts water

2 bay leaves
2 sprigs parsley
¼ teaspoon whole black peppercorns
¼ cup uncooked rice
3 large onions, peeled
2 tablespoons butter
1¾ teaspoons salt
2 ounces apricot leather (or substitute tart dried apricots)
¼ cup boiling water
1 tablespoon lemon juice
Freshly ground black pepper
2 garlic cloves, peeled and minced
¼ teaspoon cayenne
¼ teaspoon paprika
Generous ½ teaspoon *each* ground coriander seed, dried basil,
    ground caraway seed, and ground marigold
3 tablespoons finely chopped fresh herbs (cilantro, parsley, dill)

Bring the beef and bones to a boil in the 2 quarts water and skim the foam that rises to the surface. Then add the bay leaves, parsley sprigs, and peppercorns and simmer for 1½ hours. Strain, reserving meat.

Return the broth to a boil, add the rice, and simmer for 10 minutes.

Meanwhile, finely chop the onions and cook in the butter until soft but not brown. Add them to the soup along with the salt. Cook 10 minutes more, or until the rice is done.

Put the apricot leather in a bowl and pour the ¼ cup boiling water over it. Let stand for 15 minutes, then stir until creamy. (If using dried apricots, purée them. They should not be in pieces.) Add the lemon juice.

Return the meat to the pot. Stir in the freshly ground pepper, the garlic, cayenne, paprika, ground spices, and apricot purée. Cook for 10 minutes more. (The soup may be cooled and refrigerated at this point. When ready to serve, heat gently, then proceed with the recipe.)

Stir in the fresh herbs and let the soup stand for 5 minutes before serving.

# LEMONY CHICKEN SOUP
## (Chikhirtma)

One of the best descriptions of the Georgian proclivity to rhapsodize over food is found in the novella *Is This a Man?* by the nineteenth-century writer and revolutionary Ilya Chavchavadze. Here, with considerable irony, Chavchavadze portrays the daily routines of Prince Luarsab Tatkaridze and his wife Daredzhan. The couple enjoys an unusually compatible relationship revolving mainly around food, but at times their intimacy dissolves into discord. One of their most impassioned arguments begins over the planning of the next day's meal. As Luarsab waxes poetic over the dishes he might enjoy, Daredzhan suggests *chikhirtma,* a tart chicken broth made with lemon and egg and lightly flavored with saffron. Luarsab decides he would rather eat *bozbashi,* a hearty mutton soup, and feels his masculinity threatened when Daredzhan insists that *chikhirtma* is the better pottage.

Now, from my point of view, there's no comparison between *chikhirtma* and *bozbashi.* The first is subtle and elegant, the latter rather coarse, especially when made in the traditional way Luarsab likes it, with fat from the fat-tailed sheep. Besides, *bozbashi* is an Armenian import. So I cast my vote with Daredzhan and present here a recipe for *chikhirtma.* Although the ingredients reveal a certain similarity to the famous Greek avgolemono soup made with lemon and eggs, *chikhirtma* contains no rice and is highly aromatic with spices.

SERVES 6

> One 3-pound chicken, including all the giblets except for the
>    liver
> 1 large onion, peeled
> 2 garlic cloves, peeled
> ½ teaspoon whole black peppercorns
> 4 sprigs cilantro
> 6 cups cold water
> 2 tablespoons butter
> 2 onions, peeled and finely chopped
> 1 tablespoon flour
> ½ teaspoon powdered saffron
> Generous ½ teaspoon ground cinnamon
> ½ teaspoon ground coriander seed

¾ teaspoon salt
Freshly ground black pepper
2 eggs
½ cup freshly squeezed lemon juice
Minced cilantro, basil, or dill for garnish

In a large stockpot, bring the chicken, onion, garlic, peppercorns, and cilantro to a boil in the cold water, skimming any foam that rises to the surface. Reduce heat and simmer the broth for 2½ hours, or until it is richly flavored. Strain the broth and reserve. (The chicken meat may be removed from the bones and used to make Chicken Salad, page 106.)

In a deep pot, melt the butter and sauté the chopped onion until golden. Sprinkle the flour over the onion and cook for 1 minute, stirring. Add the saffron, cinnamon, coriander, salt, and pepper; mix well. Slowly pour in the reserved chicken stock.

In a separate bowl, beat the eggs well and stir in the lemon juice. Slowly stir in about 2 cups of the hot broth. Pour the egg mixture back into the soup, stirring constantly. Simmer very gently for 1 minute to thicken slightly. Do not allow the soup to boil.

Serve garnished with minced cilantro, basil, or dill.

# HEARTY LAMB SOUP
### *(Bozbashi)*

In the event that Luarsab's desire for mutton soup piqued your interest, I now offer a recipe for *bozbashi,* with some modifications. I have substituted lamb for the mutton and omitted the extra fat used in the traditional preparation of the soup. Despite my earlier disregard, I must admit that a bowl of *bozbashi* is heartwarming on a cold night.

SERVES 4 TO 6

- 2 tablespoons butter
- 2 medium onions, chopped
- 1½ pounds lean lamb, cut into 1-inch cubes
- 1½ cups peeled, seeded, and chopped tomatoes
- 2 medium potatoes, peeled and chopped
- 1 medium red pepper, seeded and chopped
- 12 large fingers okra, trimmed and coarsely chopped
- ½ cup chopped dried apricots
- 1½ teaspoons salt
- Freshly ground black pepper
- 2 quarts water
- ¼ cup finely chopped parsley

In a large stockpot, heat the butter. Add the chopped onion and sauté until soft and golden, 10 to 15 minutes. Add the lamb and cook over medium heat, stirring occasionally, until the meat browns. Stir in the tomatoes, potatoes, red pepper, okra, apricots, salt, and pepper to taste. Cook over low heat for 5 minutes, stirring occasionally, until the vegetables begin to sweat. Add the water. Bring to a boil, then reduce the heat and simmer, covered, for 1½ hours. Stir in the parsley and serve. *Bozbashi* reheats well.

# SUMMER SOUP
## (Bostneulis Supi)

Here is another soup based on lamb, this one bursting with produce from the late summer garden. The apples and cilantro lend a hint of tartness to the broth.

SERVES 8

One ¾-pound eggplant, cut into 1-inch cubes (about 4 cups)
2 medium onions, peeled and chopped
4 tablespoons (½ stick) butter
2 pounds lamb, cut into 1½-inch pieces
¾ pound green beans, trimmed and coarsely chopped (about 3 cups)
2 large tart apples, peeled and chopped
2 teaspoons salt
Freshly ground black pepper
2 quarts water
½ cup finely chopped mixed parsley and cilantro

Sprinkle the eggplant cubes with salt and set aside to drain on paper towels for 30 minutes.

In a large stockpot, brown the onions in the butter, then add the lamb. Cook, stirring occasionally, until the lamb has browned. Add the eggplant cubes and cook over low heat, covered, for 15 minutes. Stir in the green beans, apples, salt, and pepper to taste. Add the water, bring to a boil, and simmer, covered, for 1 hour. Stir in the fresh herbs and cook for 5 minutes more.

# T R I P E   S O U P
## (Khashi)

It may come as a surprise that *khashi*, Georgia's best-loved soup, is made from tripe. At one time the Georgian nobility disdained this soup, considering it fit only for peasants. But soon they noticed that the peasants, who regularly ate *khashi* upon rising, never suffered the effects of hangovers. The nobility began to eat *khashi*, too, and now the soup is a Georgian institution. Laboratory tests have shown that the collagen in tripe does indeed counteract the effects of alcohol. My friends made other claims for the soup, assuring me that *khashi* has such therapeutic value for digestive problems that if an ulcer is diagnosed early enough, a daily serving of *khashi* can heal it in a month's time with no additional medication. I was not completely taken aback, then, when officials at the Ministry of Trade proudly handed me a copy of a document attesting to *khashi*'s curative powers. On June 5, 1961, the Presidium of the Medical Council of the Georgian Ministry of Health voted that every medical institution in Georgia be sent a recommendation to use *khashi* in the treatment of certain ailments.

*Khashi* should always be eaten early in the morning, preferably between 6:00 and 8:00 A.M. Although the etymology is uncertain, *khashi* might well take its name from the Georgian word for "bright," because the milk added at serving time turns the soup white. Some cooks mix the milk and bread in before serving the soup, but more often *khashi* is served plain with bowls of condiments so that guests can season their soup to taste at the table. While tripe soup is not for everyone, I've rarely seen Georgians eat anything with more gusto than *khashi*.

SERVES 8

½ cup suet
1 calf's foot, split
2½ pounds beef tripe
2 quarts cold water
¼ pound firm white bread, in pieces
½ cup milk
Salt
Freshly ground black pepper
4 garlic cloves, peeled and grated

If it is not already ground, grind the suet in a food processor and place in a large stockpot. Add the calf's foot and the tripe and cook, covered, over low heat until the meat begins to give off juice. Then add the water and cook the soup slowly for 5 to 6 hours, until the tripe is tender.

Soak the bread in the milk. About 10 minutes before serving the soup, remove the calf's foot. Stir into the soup the softened bread and salt and pepper to taste. Cook for 10 minutes. Pour a little broth over the grated garlic, then stir it into the soup and serve.

N O T E : Suet is available from specialty butchers year-round. During the winter, especially at Christmas, I have seen it in the supermarket meat case for use in mincemeat or birdfeed.

**Woman Milking Cow**

# RED BEAN SOUP
## (Lobios Chorba)

**B**eans were introduced from Turkey in the late sixteenth century and subsequently became a staple of Georgian cuisine. The word *chorba* also made its way to Georgia via Turkey. In Georgia, red kidney beans are most often served as a seasoned purée, but here they are coupled with vegetables and herbs to yield a thick, invigorating soup. *Lobios chorba* keeps for up to a week in the refrigerator.

SERVES 4 TO 6

> 1½ cups (½ pound) dried kidney beans
> 2 quarts water
> 1 bay leaf
> 1¼ teaspoons salt
> 2 medium onions, peeled and chopped
> 1 large carrot, peeled and finely chopped
> 2 leeks, white part only, carefully cleaned and thinly sliced
> 3 tablespoons butter
> 3 garlic cloves, peeled and roughly chopped
> 1 tablespoon *adzhika* (page 181) or 1 small hot pepper, minced
> Freshly ground black pepper
> 6 sprigs each parsley, cilantro, and dill, minced
> ⅓ cup minced celery leaf
> 1 tablespoon *tkemali* (page 119) or red wine vinegar

Place the beans in a stockpot with the water, bay leaf, and 1 teaspoon salt. Bring to a boil and boil for 2 minutes; reduce the heat and simmer until the beans are nearly tender, about 1½ hours.

Meanwhile, sauté the onions, carrot, and leeks in the butter in a skillet until soft, 15 to 20 minutes. In a mortar with a pestle, pound the garlic with the remaining ¼ teaspoon salt.

When the beans are soft, add the sautéed vegetables, the pounded garlic, the *adzhika* or minced hot pepper, and black pepper to taste. Simmer for 15 minutes more, until the beans are tender.

Stir in the minced herbs, celery leaf, and vinegar and serve.

# TOMATO SOUP WITH WALNUTS AND VERMICELLI
## (Bostneulis Kharcho)

At first glance, this soup seems quintessentially Georgian, with its ample proportions of fresh tomatoes, walnuts, and herbs. But the addition of vermicelli reveals the influence of Turkish cuisine. Georgians consider this soup a vegetarian version of the popular *kharcho*.

SERVES 6

> 4 tablespoons (½ stick) butter
> 2 medium onions, peeled and finely chopped
> 2 large garlic cloves, peeled and roughly chopped
> ½ teaspoon whole coriander seed
> ¾ teaspoon salt
> ½ teaspoon freshly ground black pepper
> 1 scant cup shelled walnuts
> 1 quart cold water
> 2 ounces vermicelli, broken into pieces (1 cup)
> 1½ pounds ripe tomatoes, chopped (see Note)
> Generous ½ cup chopped mixed parsley and cilantro

In a stockpot, heat 3 tablespoons of the butter and sauté the onions until golden. In a mortar with a pestle pound together the garlic, coriander seed, salt, and pepper. Grind the walnuts fine.

Stir the spices and nuts into the onions along with the cold water and the vermicelli. Simmer, covered, for 20 minutes.

In a separate pan, cook the tomatoes over low heat until softened. Stir them into the soup and simmer for 5 minutes more. Add the chopped herbs and the remaining 1 tablespoon of butter and simmer a few minutes longer before serving.

N O T E : If the tomatoes are not ripe enough, either add 1 teaspoon tomato paste or substitute two 16-ounce cans tomatoes, drained.

# ASPARAGUS SOUP
## (Satatsuri)

*Satatsuri* is traditionally made from the first asparagus of spring. Like *chikhirtma*, it calls for eggs to be whisked in at the last minute as a thickener, but here the eggs are allowed to curdle slightly to add texture to the soup. *Satatsuri* is light as a spring breeze, with a delicate flavor.

SERVES 4 TO 6

 1 pound asparagus, trimmed and cut into 1-inch pieces
 5 cups boiling water
 2 small onions, peeled and finely chopped
 2 tablespoons butter
 1 teaspoon salt
 Freshly ground black pepper
 2 large eggs, well beaten
 ¼ cup chopped mixed fresh herbs (parsley, cilantro, dill)

Place the asparagus in a saucepan and pour the boiling water over them. Simmer, covered, until the asparagus are fork-tender, about 5 to 8 minutes, depending on the thickness of the stalks.

Meanwhile, sauté the chopped onion in the butter. When the asparagus are done, stir in the onions, salt, and pepper to taste.

Stir a small amount of the hot broth into the beaten eggs, then carefully whisk the eggs into the soup, mixing well (the eggs are supposed to curdle slightly). Stir in the chopped herbs and simmer for a few minutes more.

# YOGURT SOUP

## *(Matsvnis Shechamandi)*

**T**his is a pleasingly tart soup, not unlike the yogurt *çorbasi* enjoyed in Turkey. Georgian yogurt soup differs from its Turkish counterpart, however, in that water is used for the base instead of meat broth, making it appropriate for a vegetarian diet.

SERVES 4

> 1 tablespoon flour
> ⅛ teaspoon salt
> 2 cups plain yogurt
> 1 cup water
> 1 small onion, peeled and finely chopped
> 2 tablespoons butter
> 2 eggs, well beaten
> 1 tablespoon minced fresh mint
> 2 tablespoons minced cilantro
> ¼ cup cooked rice

Stir the flour and salt into the yogurt, then add the water and beat well. In a stockpot, sauté the onion lightly in the butter, then stir in the yogurt. Bring this mixture to a boil and simmer for 15 minutes. Carefully stir a little of the hot liquid into the beaten eggs, then whisk the eggs into the soup. Simmer a few minutes longer. Just before serving, add the minced herbs and rice.

# COLD FRUIT SOUP
## (Chrianteli)

**O**ne of the delicacies that reminds me most of the Kakhetian summer is a cold soup, a fresh purée of fruits with just a hint of seasoning. It takes only minutes to prepare. The fruits should be ripe enough to purée easily, but not so ripe that they are overly sweet. Unlike the more familiar fruit soups of northern and central Europe, *chrianteli* has no added sweeteners or thickening agents.

SERVES 4

> 2 pounds cherries or blackberries
> 3 sprigs each cilantro and dill, coarse stems removed
> ⅛ teaspoon salt
> ½ small garlic clove, peeled and pressed
> Minced scallion and cucumber for garnish

If using cherries, stem and pit them. Put the fruit through a food mill. Mince the cilantro and dill. Mix the puréed fruit with the salt, garlic, and herbs. Chill lightly. Garnish each bowl with minced scallion and cucumber.

# MEAT

**M**any different kinds of meat and game are enjoyed in Georgia, from beef to kid to wild boar. Until this century and the advent of modern agriculture, however, meat was considered a luxury, hardly daily fare. For this reason numerous ways were devised to preserve the freshly slaughtered animal. Apart from eating the meat fresh, Georgians salted, dried, and smoked it, sometimes in a *toné* or clay oven. In the mountains, shepherds chilled meat by placing it under the running water of cold alpine streams. One ancient method of preserving meat, still practiced in some regions, is to place it in an oxskin, boil the skin in a large kettle, and then bury it deep in the ground. This meat (*gudis kaurma*) keeps for up to a year. Today most meat is consumed fresh, and the Georgian culinary repertoire is replete with mouth-watering grills and stews.

## VEAL STEW WITH TOMATOES AND HERBS
### (Buglama)

**O**ne of the most famous dishes of Kakheti is *buglama,* from a Turkish word meaning "steamed." In its most basic version *buglama* is simply boiled beef flavored with dill and garlic, traditionally served at funeral repasts. But *buglama* can also be made from veal or fish and served on other occasions. I first tasted *buglama* in Telavi, Kakheti's commercial center, at a café in the former Esperanto Hotel. Our host was Luka Nikashvili, head of catering for the city, who arranged for his chefs to show me around their infernally hot kitchen in the building's basement. Although we had appeared on short notice, our new friends insisted we stay for an impromptu feast in the middle of the day. We agreed with some hesitation, not yet aware of the extremes of Georgian hospitality. It turned out that we were held hostage until after breakfast the next day, so that we could try all of the Kakhetian specialties that the chefs could concoct for us.

Luka was eager to explain how seriously Kakhetians take the preparation of *buglama*. He told an anecdote about a little boy who everyone thought was dumb because by the age of four he still hadn't uttered a word. One day, though, while eating his *buglama*, the little boy spoke, declaring, "This doesn't have enough salt." Everyone was stunned and excitedly cried, "But if you can talk, why haven't you spoken before?" The little boy replied in all seriousness: "Until today, the *buglama* was always properly seasoned."

Kakhetians emphasize the importance of judicious seasoning, aphoristically saying that "if you do a good deed, don't forget to put some salt on it"—in other words, make it even better. In the *buglama* recipe that follows, savor and fragrance are provided by an abundance of tomatoes and fresh herbs.

**SERVES 6 TO 8**

> 2 tablespoons butter
> 3½ pounds stewing veal, cut into 2-inch pieces
> Salt and freshly ground black pepper to taste
> 2 pounds ripe tomatoes, quartered
> 2 medium onions, peeled and sliced
> ½ cup chopped mixed fresh herbs (dill, basil, tarragon, cilantro)
> 1 large bay leaf
> ¼ cup water

Heat the butter in a dutch oven and add half the meat. Sprinkle with salt and pepper. Layer half the tomatoes, onions, and herbs over the meat. Repeat the layering with the remaining ingredients. Add the bay leaf and pour in the water. Cover, bring to a boil, and simmer gently for 1½ hours, until the meat is tender. Plain boiled rice is a good accompaniment to *buglama*.

# BEEF STEW
## (*Sousi*)

*Sousi* is a spicy stew that is prepared in a rather unorthodox manner. One would expect that steaming the beef and then cooking it over high heat would toughen it, but the meat turns out remarkably tender. Chock-full of vegetables, *sousi* makes an excellent one-dish meal. Serve with a crusty bread to soak up the juices.

SERVES 4 TO 6

> 2 pounds stewing beef, cut into 1-inch cubes
> 10 tablespoons (1¼ sticks) butter
> 3 medium onions, peeled and coarsely chopped
> 2 pounds potatoes, peeled and coarsely chopped
> 2 pounds tomatoes, peeled and seeded (or two 28-ounce cans, drained)
> 2 bay leaves
> 4 cups chopped cilantro (¼ pound)
> 4 cups chopped basil (¼ pound)
> 1 green pepper, chopped
> 1 hot red or green pepper, chopped
> 1 teaspoon salt
> 1 cup water
> Freshly ground black pepper

Place the meat in a dutch oven and cook, covered, over low heat until it begins to sweat. Without adding any liquid, braise the meat for about 10 minutes, stirring once. Uncover the pan and turn the heat to high. Cook for another 10 minutes, until the liquid evaporates.

Add the butter at this point, and cook the meat over medium high heat for about 10 minutes more, stirring occasionally, until it browns. Next, add the onions and potatoes and cook for 5 more minutes.

Purée the tomatoes and add to the pan along with the remaining ingredients, seasoning to taste with pepper. Mix well. Simmer, covered, for 1 hour.

# BEEF STEW WITH PICKLES
## (Solyanka)

*Solyanka* is another piquant beef stew. Russians consider it Georgian because it has a bite, but actually *solyanka* is a Georgian adaptation of an originally Russian stew (the dill pickles give it away). Served with freshly cooked *mchadi* or corncakes (page 149), *solyanka* makes a robust meal, best suited for autumn or wintertime dining.

SERVES 4

  2 pounds top round of beef, cut into 1½-inch cubes
  Salt and freshly ground black pepper
  2 tablespoons flour
  3 tablespoons butter
  2 medium onions, peeled and coarsely chopped
  3 garlic cloves, peeled and minced
  ½ cup tomato purée
  1 tablespoon picante sauce (Worcestershire sauce mixed with hot
    pepper sauce, or a prepared sauce like Pickapeppa)
  1 bay leaf
  1½ cups coarsely chopped sour dill pickles
  2 heaping tablespoons capers
  1½ tablespoons red wine vinegar
  ¾ cup water

Preheat the oven to 300° F.

Season the meat with salt and pepper, then sprinkle with the flour.

Heat the butter in a large ovenproof casserole. Sauté the meat until it browns. Stir in the onions and garlic and cook for 10 minutes.

Add in the remaining ingredients, mixing well. Cover the casserole and braise in the oven for 2 hours, or until the meat is tender.

# BEEF PATTIES
## (Gupta)

These Georgian-style hamburgers, eaten plain without bread, are fruity with raisins. Arranged in radiating circles on a platter, *gupta* make an elegant entrée for the buffet table.

SERVES 3 OR 4

> ¾ pound stewing beef (or use leftover cooked beef)
> 4 tablespoons (½ stick) butter
> 1 cup raisins
> 1 medium potato, boiled
> ½ cup shelled walnuts
> ¼ cup chopped parsley
> ¾ teaspoon salt
> Freshly ground black pepper
> 1 egg, well beaten
> ⅓ cup fine dry bread crumbs
> Parsley sprigs, for garnish

Bring the beef to a boil in cold salted water, skimming any foam that rises to the surface. Simmer, partially covered, for 1 hour, or until tender.

In a skillet melt 2 tablespoons of the butter. Stir in ¾ cup of the raisins and cook them, covered, over low heat until plump, about 10 minutes.

In a food processor, coarsely grind together the boiled beef, potato, walnuts, the remaining ¼ cup raisins, and the parsley. Stir in the salt, pepper to taste, and beaten egg. Shape the mixture into 12 flat, oval patties, about 3 inches long. Dust the patties with bread crumbs.

Melt the remaining 2 tablespoons butter in a large skillet and fry the patties slowly until browned, turning once. Arrange the patties decoratively on a platter and strew the plumped raisins over them. Garnish with sprigs of parsley.

# STUFFED QUINCE
## (*Komshis Tolma*)

**S**tuffed vegetables are popular throughout Georgia. While filled grape leaves are closely associated with Turkish cuisine, in Georgia you're as likely to eat stuffed quince, tomatoes, or eggplant. In a departure from Turkish practice, rice is rarely used as the main filling component. It serves instead as a binding ingredient, as in the following recipe for stuffed quince with meat. The combination of fruit and meat yields a wonderful sweet-sour flavor. Try this dish in the autumn, when quince are in season.

SERVES 6

- ¾ pound beef sirloin
- 2 tablespoons minced fresh tarragon, or 1 teaspoon dried
- 2 tablespoons minced fresh dill, or 1 teaspoon dried
- Pinch ground coriander seed
- Pinch ground cinnamon
- ½ teaspoon salt
- ¼ teaspoon freshly ground black pepper
- 2 tablespoons cooked rice (it should be al dente)
- 6 quince
- 2 tablespoons butter
- 1 garlic clove, peeled and minced
- 1 small onion, peeled and minced
- 2½ cups beef broth
- ¾ cup coarsely chopped dried apricots

Finely mince the beef by hand or in a food processor. Do not grind it. (The dish will taste best if you include some of the fat.) In a large skillet cook the minced beef until just brown, then stir in the tarragon, dill, coriander, cinnamon, salt, pepper, and cooked rice. Set aside.

Cut a ½-inch slice off the stem end of each quince and set aside. Scoop out the cores to within ½ inch of the bottom. With a spoon remove some of the pulp, leaving about a ¼-inch shell. Dice the pulp from 4 of the quince.

In another skillet melt the butter and add the garlic, onion, and diced quince. Sauté over medium heat for about 10 minutes, stirring occasionally, until the mixture softens. Check for seasoning. Stir this mixture into the meat.

Pack the filling firmly into the quince and cover each quince with its own lid. Place the fruit in a deep pan and pour the beef broth around it. Add the dried apricots. Cover and simmer for 45 minutes. Serve with the broth and dried apricots.

# LIVER WITH POMEGRANATE JUICE
## *(Ghvidzli)*

Although many traditional Georgian foods take a long time to prepare, Georgian cooks do not mind spending long hours in the kitchen, since it affords them a chance to socialize—rare is the cook who labors alone. For quick family meals, however, dishes that don't demand any fuss are appreciated. One of these is calf's liver, which must be cooked quickly to remain tender. The liver should be so fresh that it virtually melts in the mouth. To balance the richness of the meat, Georgians often cook it with vinegar or tomatoes. I find the liver especially pleasing with pomegranate juice.

In the recipe offered here, no complicated preparations are necessary. Simply squeeze a fresh pomegranate for juice and add it to the pan.

SERVES 2 OR 3

    1 pound calf's liver, in 4 slices
    3 tablespoons butter
    ½ cup freshly squeezed pomegranate juice (or substitute
        unsweetened bottled juice)
    2 tablespoons minced cilantro
    Salt
    Freshly ground black pepper

Fry the liver quickly in the butter. To the pomegranate juice add the cilantro and salt and pepper to taste. When the liver is done, transfer it to a warm serving dish. Add the pomegranate juice to the fat remaining in the pan. Boil for a minute or two to thicken slightly. Pour the sauce over the liver and serve at once.

# MARINATED GRILLED MEAT
## (Basturma)

The most common grill in Georgia is *mtsvadi*, skewers of plain, freshly slaughtered lamb, beef, or pork. If the meat is less tender, however, it can be marinated overnight before grilling, in which case it is known as *basturma*. As a culinary term, *basturma* is related to *basderma* and *pastirma*, the Armenian and Turkish words for spiced dried beef (our word for spiced cooked beef, *pastrami*, is also related). But Georgians use *basturma* to refer exclusively to grilled meat.

The following recipes call specifically for lamb and beef, but the marinades are interchangeable and work equally well with pork.

## BASTURMA OF LAMB

SERVES 4 TO 6

> 2 cups pomegranate juice
> ¼ cup olive oil
> 1 teaspoon salt
> Freshly ground black pepper
> 1 bay leaf, crushed
> 2 garlic cloves, peeled and crushed
> 2 pounds boneless shoulder or leg of lamb, cut into 2-inch cubes
> One 1-pound eggplant, salted, drained, and parboiled (optional)

Mix together the pomegranate juice, olive oil, salt, pepper to taste, bay leaf, and garlic. Marinate the lamb overnight in this mixture. The following day, place the meat on skewers, alternating (if desired) with eggplant cubes.

Grill over hot coals for about 10 minutes. Serve with *tkemali* sauce (page 119).

# BASTURMA OF BEEF

2 pounds boneless beef sirloin, cut into 2-inch cubes
1 large onion, peeled and grated
1 teaspoon salt
3 black peppercorns, crushed
2 garlic cloves, peeled and crushed
2 tablespoons chopped cilantro
1 tablespoon chopped fresh basil
1¼ cups olive oil
¾ cup freshly squeezed lemon juice
Tomatoes, scallions

Place the meat cubes in a large bowl. Mix together thoroughly the onion, salt, peppercorns, garlic, and herbs. Combine the olive oil and lemon juice, and stir in the onion mixture. Pour over the meat. Marinate overnight, preferably for 24 hours.

Put the cubes on skewers and grill over hot coals for about 10 minutes, turning once. The meat should still be pink inside.

Serve garnished with tomato wedges and scallions. Cilantro sauce (page 121) and tomato sauce (page 122) are particularly good with this dish.

# LAMB AND VEGETABLE STEW
## (Chanakhi)

*Chanakhi* is an earthy stew braised slowly in a clay pot to ensure that the flavors of meat and vegetables deepen and meld. Georgians like to prepare *chanakhi* in individual pots, taking care that each serving contains an assortment of vegetables; however, a large, family-style casserole may also be used. *Chanakhi* needs no accompaniment other than bread and perhaps a wedge of cheese.

SERVES 4

8 tablespoons (1 stick) butter
5 garlic cloves
1 large hot red or green pepper
4 cups chopped cilantro (¼ pound)
4 cups chopped basil (¼ pound)
1½ pounds lean lamb, cut into 2-inch cubes
Salt and freshly ground black pepper
4 medium onions, peeled and cut into eighths
¾ pound eggplant, unpeeled and cubed
1 pound potatoes, peeled and cubed
1 pound tomatoes, coarsely chopped
6 tablespoons water

Preheat oven to 300° F.

Melt the butter in a 3-quart casserole (preferably earthenware). Coarsely grind together the garlic, hot pepper, cilantro, and basil. Place half the lamb in the casserole and season with salt and pepper. Layer half the onions, eggplant, potatoes, ground herbs, and tomatoes on top of the meat. Repeat with the remaining ingredients, keeping them in separate layers. Pour in the water, cover the casserole, and braise slowly in the oven for 4½ to 5 hours.

VARIATION

The presentation of *chanakhi* is particularly nice if you use small vegetables, substituting cherry tomatoes for large ones and small eggplants for globes. The small eggplants are stuffed with the herbs, making each bite of the vegetable particularly succulent. To use small eggplants, slit them lengthwise and stuff them with the ground herb mixture, instead of layering these ingredients separately.

# B R A I S E D    L A M B    C H O P S
## *(C h a k a p u l i)*

*Chakapuli* is another popular slow-cooked dish. It can be made with almost any meat, although lamb or kid is preferred. This sort of liquidy stew is popular in Georgia. The meat is eaten separately, then the broth drunk like soup. Redolent with herbs and pungent with the fruity flavors of wine and *tkemali* sauce, *chakapuli* for me captures the essential taste of Georgia. Serve this stew with bread and mild cheese.

SERVES 4 TO 6

    2 pounds shoulder lamb chops
    3 onions, peeled and chopped
    1 cup dry white wine
    ½ cup *tkemali* sauce (page 119)
    3 cups loosely packed fresh tarragon leaves
    1 cup loosely packed mixed fresh herbs (parsley, mint, dill,
        cilantro)
    1 large garlic clove, peeled and minced
    ½ teaspoon salt

Preheat the oven to 350° F.

Place the lamb chops in a single layer in a flameproof casserole and top with the chopped onions. Pour on the white wine. Cover the casserole and bring to a boil. Transfer to the oven and braise the lamb until tender, about 1½ hours.

Coarsely chop the fresh herbs. When the lamb is ready, stir in the *tkemali* sauce, the herbs, the minced garlic, and the salt. Return the casserole to the oven and cook 5 minutes longer. Let the lamb sit 5 minutes before serving.

# LAMB WITH GREEN BEANS
## (Mtsvane Lobio Batknis Khortsit)

This dish could easily be classified under vegetables. Against expectation, the lamb plays second fiddle to the beans, the cubes of meat serving almost as garnish for an aromatic purée of beans and herbs. Even though it contains no fats, this version of *lobio* is rich and substantial.

SERVES 4

> 1 pound boneless shoulder or leg of lamb, cut into 1½-inch pieces
> 2 onions, peeled and chopped
> 1 teaspoon salt
> Freshly ground black pepper
> 1½ pounds green beans, trimmed and cut into 1-inch pieces
> ½ cup boiling water
> 1 cup packed fresh basil leaves, chopped
> ¼ cup packed fresh summer savory, chopped

Place the lamb in a dutch oven, cover, and steam in its own juices over low heat for 10 to 15 minutes. Add the onions, salt, and pepper to taste and continue to cook, covered, until the onions are soft, about 15 minutes. Add the green beans, placing them in a separate layer on top of the meat and onions. Do not stir. Pour in the boiling water and simmer, covered, until the beans are soft. Depending on the age and thickness of the beans, this could take anywhere from 20 minutes to 1 hour.

When the beans are soft, carefully remove them from the pan and purée in a food processor. Stir the bean purée back into the lamb, and simmer for 5 minutes more. Stir in the chopped herbs and serve.

# RICE PILAF
## (Shilaplavi)

Georgians enjoy many different varieties of *shilaplavi* or pilaf, a borrowing from Persian cuisine. Persian recipes regularly mix rice with lentils, beans, fruits, vegetables, or meats; the Georgians favor combinations of their own. In one of the best local pilafs, potatoes are added to the rice and the dish is flavored with caraway. This variation can be classified as a "white" pilaf, according to the categories named by Chardin, who savored Georgian pilafs several centuries ago. At one feast he describes an entire course consisting of nothing but various pilafs. Each course offered sixty dishes, or so he claimed, including yellow pilaf boiled with sugar, cinnamon, and saffron, red pilaf boiled with pomegranate juice, and white pilaf, which he considered the most natural and wholesome.

Chardin is serious when he mentions the wholesomeness of rice. Further on in his travel notes he records a novel cure for "the Yellow Jaundice": "Make a Bed of Boyl'd Rice, and lay the Patient well cover'd upon it." While I would rather eat this pilaf than lie in it, I may be missing something.

SERVES 6 TO 8

> 1 pound lamb, cut into 1½-inch pieces
> 1 teaspoon salt
> ½ teaspoon caraway seed
> 2 large onions, peeled and finely chopped
> 1 cup uncooked rice
> 2 cups water
> 4 tablespoons (½ stick) butter
> 2 medium potatoes, cut into 1-inch cubes
> ¼ cup chopped parsley
> Freshly ground black pepper

Place the lamb in a dutch oven with ½ teaspoon of the salt. Cover the pan and cook the lamb over low heat until it gives off juice, 10 to 15 minutes. Stir in the caraway seed and chopped onions and cook, uncovered, over medium heat until the onions are golden.

Meanwhile, simmer the rice in 1 cup of the water for 10 minutes, or until the water is absorbed.

*(Continued)*

In a stockpot, melt the butter. Place the potatoes in the pot in a single layer. Top them with half of the rice, then on top of the rice place the meat mixture. Add the remaining ½ teaspoon salt, pepper to taste, and the chopped parsley. Top with the remaining rice and pour the remaining 1 cup water over all.

Wet a linen dishtowel and place it over the top of the pot, then cover with the lid. Steam the dish gently for 1 hour, or until tender.

Shepherd with Flock

# MEATLOAF
## (Chizhi-Pizhi)

For a quick meal, try this Georgian-style meatloaf. Its humorous name probably derives from a popular Russian ditty about a siskin, a small finch. If millions of English-speaking children ask, "Pussycat, pussycat, where have you been?," then the Russian counterpart, "*Chizhik-pyzhik*, where have you been?," is not for children alone. It turns out that this little bird has been to the Fontanka River in St. Petersburg, where he drank enough vodka to mix him up and make his head spin. In a playful linguistic borrowing, the bird's name has been Georgianized into *chizhi-pizhi* and applied to a mixed-up combination of ingredients. As long as you savor this meatloaf without vodka, your head should not spin.

SERVES 2 TO 4

    1 small onion, peeled and minced
    1 large garlic clove, peeled and minced
    2 tablespoons butter
    1 pound lean ground lamb or beef
    ¾ teaspoon salt
    Freshly ground black pepper
    ¼ cup chopped mixed fresh dill and parsley
    Pinch salt
    2 eggs, beaten

Preheat the oven to 350° F. Grease two shallow 6-inch casseroles.

Lightly sauté the onion and garlic in the butter, then mix with the ground meat along with the salt and pepper to taste. Divide the mixture and press it into the prepared dishes.

Whisk the chopped herbs and pinch of salt into the beaten eggs, then pour the eggs over the meat mixture. Bake for 30 minutes.

# ROAST SUCKLING PIG
## (Gochi)

Of all meats, Georgians most enjoy beef the year round, considering pork a wintertime pleasure and lamb best in the spring. Their preference for the tender meat of very young animals has given rise to jokes about how the Georgians undermined Soviet production quotas by eating the animals before they even had a chance to be counted. In fact, the Georgian culinary vocabulary differentiates among animals at different stages of growth. At New Year's the Georgians particularly like to eat *gochi* or suckling pig, which the markets offer at a tender weight of ten to fourteen pounds, as compared to the twenty-pound pigs commonly found here. At the New Year's feast, everyone enjoys the pig's succulent meat and crisp skin; the guest of honor is awarded the ear as a mark of esteem.

One odd use for the suckling pig is recorded by Chardin, who was given the following prescription for relief from the flu:

> The most usual Cure for Agues in this Country, is to make Plaisters of the Fat of a Sheeps Rump, Cinamon, Cloves and Cardamomes, and all the time of the cold fit to lay these Plaisters upon the Forehead, Stomach and Feet. When the hot fit is over, take off those Plaisters and lay on others, made of the Leaves of Chihory, Plantain, and the Herb call'd Solanum or Nightshade, afterwards they take a Suckling-Pig, cut it in two and clap it to the Feet. All which time the Patient is fed with Bread and Cream of Almonds, eating nothing that is boyl'd.
>
> —*The Travels of Sir John Chardin into Persia and the East-Indies . . . (1686)*

To my mind, suckling pig is much better applied to fits of hunger than to fits of fever or chills, but to each his own temper.

To prepare a suckling pig in the Georgian manner, rub it all over with the following spice mixture and then roast in the oven or on a spit over an open fire, using a drip pan to catch the juices. For every four pounds of meat, use these proportions of spice mixture:

**3 tablespoons boiling water**
**4 teaspoons whole black peppercorns**
**3 or 4 teaspoons hot red pepper flakes**

4 teaspoons whole coriander seed
2 teaspoons dried summer savory
8 large garlic cloves, peeled and roughly chopped
4 teaspoons salt
2 tablespoons walnut oil

Pour the boiling water over the peppercorns and red pepper flakes and leave until softened, about 30 minutes. In a mortar with a pestle, pound them together with the coriander seed and savory. Add the garlic and salt and continue pounding until a paste is formed. Stir in the walnut oil.

A couple of hours before placing the pig in the oven, rub it all over with this mixture, rubbing a little on the inside, too. Roast at 350° F., about 15 minutes to the pound, for 2½ hours, basting frequently. After carving, pour the pan juices over the sliced meat.

N O T E : This spice rub is also excellent on roast chicken.

Family Picnicking

# SPICY MEATBALLS
## (Abkhazura)

One of the liveliest preparations from Abkhazia on the Black Sea coast is *abkhazura*, highly seasoned meatballs served with *tkemali* sauce. Extra flavor is imparted to the meatballs by wrapping them in lacy caul fat, which also enhances their appearance. But since caul fat is often hard to find here, the meatballs may be shaped without it. This invigorating recipe comes from Marina Mirianashvili.

SERVES 8

> 1 pound pork butt
> ¾ pound beef chuck
> 1 small onion, peeled
> 4 large garlic cloves, peeled
> ½ to ¾ teaspoon cayenne
> ½ teaspoon freshly ground black pepper
> ½ teaspoon ground coriander seed
> ½ teaspoon dried fenugreek
> ½ teaspoon dried summer savory
> 2 teaspoons salt
> 2 tablespoons ground barberry or sumac
> 1 pound caul fat, if available
> Vinegar

Grind together the pork, beef, onion, and garlic. Work the spices in well with your hands. (Stirring with a spoon will not blend the flavors sufficiently.)

Soak the caul fat in warm water with a little vinegar until it becomes pliable, then cut it into 4-inch squares. Place a mound of ground meat mixture on each square and enclose it in the fat to make a plump meatball. Fry the meatballs over low heat until cooked through and nicely browned. Serve with *tkemali* sauce (page 119).

# GEORGIAN SAUSAGE
## (Kupati)

Traditional breakfasts in Kakheti, as in America, are often hearty. For daily fare, families usually opt for light foods such as yogurt, cheese, olives, and fruit, but when guests arrive, they prepare a substantial meal revolving around meat. Yogurt and bread merely enhance such steaming dishes as *kupati* or coiled sausages, aromatic with cinnamon and cloves. Try scrambled eggs with *kupati* for breakfast, in place of our usual link sausages. I happen to like *kupati* best for dinner, hot from the grill and accompanied by an assortment of vegetables.

To be authentic, the ground meat and spices for *kupati* should be stuffed into sausage casings, but since casings are often unavailable, I find that *kupati* taste equally good when simply shaped into patties, even if they look mundane. As patties, *kupati* take surprisingly little time to prepare.

SERVES 4

> 1 pound pork butt
> ½ pound hard fatback (or salt pork, blanched for 15 minutes
>     and chilled)
> 2 large garlic cloves, peeled
> 1 teaspoon dried summer savory
> ½ teaspoon ground cinnamon
> ⅛ teaspoon ground cloves
> 1 teaspoon freshly ground black pepper
> 2 teaspoons salt
> ¼ cup *tkemali* sauce (see page 119)

Grind together medium-fine the pork butt, fatback, and garlic. Thoroughly work in the spices with your hands, then stir in the *tkemali* sauce. Stuff the mixture into casings to make sausages about 1½ inches in diameter. Tie the casings at 8-inch intervals, tying off each link twice so that they can be cut apart. Separate the links and shape into horseshoes or coils. Either grill or fry the *kupati* in a skillet.

If casings are unavailable, the prepared sausage meat may simply be shaped into patties before cooking.

# COLD JELLIED PORK
## (Muzhuzhi)

*Muzhuzhi* is a favorite Georgian dish that exists in both hot and cold versions. I have chosen to present the cold dish here, because many people are squeamish about eating pig's feet. In this version, the feet are removed before serving, having already imparted the necessary body and flavor to the broth. Cold *muzhuzhi* is particularly refreshing in the summer heat.

SERVES 10 TO 12

> 2 pig's feet (about 1 pound)
> 1 pound pork butt
> 2 onions, peeled, each stuck with 4 cloves
> 2 carrots, peeled
> 2 garlic cloves, peeled
> ¼ teaspoon whole allspice berries
> A 2-inch piece stick cinnamon
> ½ teaspoon whole black peppercorns
> 2 bay leaves
> 6 cups cold water
> ½ cup white wine vinegar
> Salt

Place the pig's feet, meat, vegetables, and spices in a large stockpot. Pour on the cold water and vinegar and bring to a boil. Simmer gently for 6 hours, then strain the broth into a clean saucepan. Boil the broth until it is reduced by half. Test for seasoning, adding salt to taste.

While the broth is reducing, shred the pork butt and place in a deep serving dish. Pour the reduced broth over the meat and allow to cool. Chill until firm, 6 to 8 hours.

N O T E : The Georgians serve *muzhuzhi* with a fine layer of chilled fat on top. If you wish to eliminate this layer, the reduced broth may be chilled and skimmed of fat. Reheat it before pouring over the meat.

# POULTRY

**A**ll over rural Georgia, an enchanting scene occurs each evening at twilight. Chickens that range freely about the farmsteads stop clucking. As the sky grows dim, they fly up into the trees to roost, their wings whishing. The crepuscular sky and the sudden stillness of dozens of birds in *tkemali* trees create a strangely beautiful sight.

Since chickens in Georgia are not kept in coops, their meat tastes especially flavorful. Ducks, geese, and turkeys also roam at will, ever at risk for the evening meal. Some variety of domestic or wild fowl is a featured ingredient in several signature dishes of Georgian cuisine: *tabaka,* flattened grilled chicken with a pungent garlic or plum sauce; *satsivi,* turkey bathed in a lush nut sauce; or *chakhokhbili,* a savory stew with tomatoes and herbs.

## TURKEY SATSIVI
### (Indauris Satsivi)

*Satsivi* is a good place to begin an excursion into Georgian ways with poultry, since it is encountered at nearly every feast. While there are over a dozen varieties of Georgian nut sauces, *satsivi* is the most renowned. It may be served with poultry, fish, or vegetables. In each case the ingredients are adjusted to best suit the food that the sauce complements. For instance, poultry *satsivi* uses broth from the boiled bird as the liquid base. When fish or vegetables are used, the broth changes accordingly.

Like other Georgian nut sauces, *satsivi* differs from such Balkan and Turkish preparations as *tarator* and Circassian chicken in that bread is never added for binding—Georgians consider nuts binding enough. After the sauce has cooked, the prepared bird is immersed in it, then allowed to cool to room temperature. This cooling process thickens the sauce. It also gives the dish its name, as *satsivi* derives from the word *tsivi* or "cold."

SERVES 6 TO 8

**1 young 6- to 7-pound turkey (or substitute a roasting hen)**
**2 bay leaves**
**4 sprigs parsley**
**6 cups water**

**4 tablespoons (½ stick) butter**
**3 onions, peeled and chopped**
**2 heaping cups shelled walnuts**
**6 garlic cloves, peeled**
**1½ teaspoons ground cinnamon**
**½ teaspoon ground cloves**
**1½ teaspoons ground coriander seed**
**1½ teaspoons ground marigold**
**1¼ teaspoons freshly ground black pepper**
**½ teaspoon paprika**
**¼ teaspoon cayenne**
**¾ teaspoon salt**
**¼ cup red wine vinegar**

Place the turkey in a stockpot and add the bay leaves, parsley, and water. Bring to a boil, cover, and simmer for 45 minutes.

Preheat the oven to 350° F.

Remove the turkey to a roasting pan, reserving the stock. Roast for 45 minutes, basting occasionally with the pan juices, until golden. Cut into small pieces and place them in a serving dish.

While the turkey is roasting, measure the reserved stock. Cook, uncovered, over medium heat to reduce to 4 cups. Set aside.

Next, prepare the sauce. In a heavy skillet, melt the butter and add the chopped onions. Sauté until transparent.

Grind the walnuts together with the garlic, then add to the onions, stirring well. Return this mixture to the food processor or meat grinder and grind again to make a paste. Place the paste in the skillet and stir in the remaining ingredients except for the vinegar. Continue to cook over low heat, stirring, for a few minutes. Gradually pour in the 4 cups reserved stock. Cook over low heat, stirring occasionally, for 20 minutes, then stir in the wine vinegar. (The sauce will not be very thick.)

Pour the sauce over the turkey and allow the *satsivi* to cool. Serve at room temperature.

N O T E : For traditional *satsivi,* the meat is left on the bones. For ease of serving at an American-style buffet, where it is difficult to manage knife and fork, the meat may be cut from the bones into small pieces.

Some cooks like to enrich the *satsivi* with an egg yolk or two stirred in at the end of the cooking time. I find the egg version unnecessarily rich, however.

**Still Life**

# CHICKEN BAZHE
## (Katmis Bazhe)

Tradition holds that *satsivi* is a cool-weather dish, as food left sitting out in the heat could spoil. But even in summer, the Georgians do not want to forgo their poultry with nut sauces entirely, so during the sweltering months they prepare a much simpler variety, called *bazhe*. This sauce is most often served with roasted fowl; unlike *satsivi*, it is poured over the cooked meat at serving time. Requiring only ground nuts, water, and spices, *bazhe* is quicker to prepare than *satsivi*, although the nuts are still painstakingly pounded.

SERVES 6

1½ cups walnuts
5 garlic cloves, peeled and roughly chopped
¾ cup boiling water
2 teaspoons red wine vinegar
½ teaspoon salt
1 teaspoon ground marigold
¾ teaspoon ground coriander seeds
¼ teaspoon paprika
Dash cayenne
One 4- to 5-pound roasting chicken
Butter or olive oil

In a food processor, grind the nuts coarsely. Add the garlic and continue to grind to a paste. Transfer to a bowl and beat in the boiling water, stirring constantly until smooth. Stir in the vinegar and spices. Allow to sit for several hours to meld.

About 1½ hours before serving time, rinse the chicken and wipe it dry. Rub the skin with a little butter or olive oil. Place on a rack in a shallow pan and roast at 375° F. for 1 to 1¼ hours, basting occasionally. Remove the chicken from the oven and allow to sit for 10 minutes before carving.

Serve the *bazhe* sauce over slices of hot roast chicken.

# GARLIC FRIED CHICKEN
## (Chkmeruli)

Another recipe for chicken comes from Tokhliauri, a cooperative restaurant in Tbilisi that specializes in western Georgian food. Here, walnuts are paired with chicken in yet another rendition of nut sauce. Where *bazhe* is basic and *satsivi* refined, *chkmeruli* is gutsy. This is a hearty, family-style dish that takes very little effort to prepare.

SERVES 3 OR 4

 One 3-pound chicken, cut into pieces
 Salt
 Freshly ground black pepper
 2 tablespoons butter
 1 tablespoon vegetable oil
 10 to 12 garlic cloves, peeled
 1 cup walnuts
 1 cup water

Season the chicken pieces with salt and pepper.

In a large skillet, heat the butter and oil. Fry the chicken over medium high heat for 10 minutes; turn and fry for 10 minutes more. Cover the pan and continue cooking over low heat for 20 to 25 minutes, until the chicken is done.

Meanwhile, finely grind together the garlic and walnuts.

When the chicken is tender, transfer it to a plate and keep warm. Pour off all but 4 tablespoons of the pan drippings. Add the ground garlic and nuts to the fat remaining in the pan, along with the water. Sprinkle on about ¼ teaspoon more salt. Simmer for 5 minutes. Return the chicken to the pan, turning it to coat well with the sauce. Heat thoroughly before serving.

# FLATTENED CHICKEN
## (Tabaka)

In Georgia, chicken rivals beef for year-round popularity. The Georgians either slaughter the birds themselves or buy them at the farmers' market, from young poussins to boiling hens to cocks. One of the best-loved ways to prepare young chicken is to bone it partially and flatten it, then fry it under a heavy weight. This is the famous chicken *tabaka,* which has become such a standard of Russian restaurant cuisine that you're as likely to eat it in Moscow as in Tbilisi. The name comes from the special heavy skillet or *tapha* that is used. For indoor cooking the skillet is usually cast-iron, but for the open fire a *ketsi* or red clay dish is preferred. The weights can be heavy cans from the cupboard or flat river stones, depending on where the cooking is taking place.

The simplest way to present *tabaka* is with the sharp plum sauce, *tkemali.* In one of my favorite versions, *tabaka* is served with *niortskali,* a pungent garlic sauce, and *borani,* green beans flavored lightly with cinnamon and mixed with yogurt. The traditional method calls for layering the chicken and green beans. I hate to shroud the beautiful chickens in yogurt and prefer instead to serve them on a large platter surrounded by the beans, with some sauce ladled on top. This makes a festive and colorful dish.

*PER SERVING*
>One 1- to 1½-pound squab or rock cornish game hen
>1 garlic clove, peeled and crushed
>Salt
>Cayenne
>2 tablespoons butter, melted

Pat the hen dry and place it breast side up on a large cutting board. With a sharp knife, slice down the middle of the breast bone, to separate the rib cage. Be careful not to cut all the way through the hen —it should remain in one piece. Turn the hen over and flatten it with a meat pounder.

Next, with a sharp knife make a small slit at the lower edge of each breast half and push the tips of the drumsticks through these slits, one on each side, so that the knobby ends of the drumsticks protrude on the skin side. Make similar slits on the upper edge of each breast half and push the wing tips through. Each breast half should be covered by a drumstick and wing. Flatten the hen gently once more with the meat pounder.

Rub the hen with the crushed garlic, salt liberally, and dust with cayenne.

Heat a cast-iron skillet large enough to hold the hen (two hens will fit in a 12-inch skillet). Add the butter. Once it melts put the hen in the pan, turning to coat both sides. Cook skin side up over medium high heat for 5 minutes, then turn skin side down.

Place a plate or another skillet over the hen and weight it down with a heavy can or a bowl filled with water. Cook the hen over medium heat for 20 minutes, until the skin is brown and slightly crusty. Turn, replace the weight, and cook 5 minutes more.

Serve with Garlic Sauce (page 122) and Green Bean *Borani* (page 153) or simply with *Tkemali* Sauce (page 119).

VARIATION

Though untraditional, the following method of making *tabaka* is good for a crowd, since the hens can be prepared ahead of time. Cook the hens for 5 minutes on each side as directed above. Then transfer them to a roasting pan, replace the weights, and roast in a 450° F. oven for 15 to 20 minutes.

# CHICKEN WITH HERBS
## (Chakhokhbili)

The Georgian word for pheasant is *khokhobi*, and one of the inspired dishes of Georgian cuisine is *chakhokhbili*. These days chicken, rather than pheasant, constitutes the main ingredient of *chakhokhbili*, but the manner of preparation has not changed. The fowl is simmered with vegetables and herbs until tender, with no liquid added. Just as Georgian boys were once judged by their skill in cutting *mtsvadi* sticks, so Georgian girls were deemed marriageable according to their ability to cut up chicken for *chakhokhbili*. The most traditional recipes call for seventeen precise pieces, although today a mere ten will suffice.

SERVES 6 TO 8

> 2 tablespoons butter
> One 3-pound chicken, cut into 10 pieces
> 4 medium onions, peeled and chopped
> 8 medium tomatoes, peeled, seeded, and coarsely chopped
> 3 garlic cloves, peeled and minced
> Generous ½ cup chopped mixed fresh herbs (parsley, cilantro, tarragon, basil, dill)
> ⅛ teaspoon dried hot red pepper flakes
> Salt
> Freshly ground black pepper

Melt the butter in a large skillet and brown the chicken pieces on all sides. Stir in the chopped onions and cook for 10 minutes, continuing to stir occasionally.

Add the prepared tomatoes and cook, covered, for 30 minutes, or until the chicken is done.

Stir in the garlic, herbs, hot pepper, and salt and pepper to taste. Cook, covered, 5 minutes longer.

Let stand 5 minutes, covered, before serving.

# GRILLED STUFFED CHICKEN
## (Shemtsvari Tsitsili Satenit)

Although red meat is considered the fare of choice for open-flame cooking, other foods are grilled as well. A whole chicken is sometimes stuffed with a mixture of *suluguni* cheese and pomegranate seeds and roasted on a spit over a slow fire, the pomegranate seeds cutting the richness of the dish. The same principle holds for chicken stuffed with rice and cherries, in which the dried fruit imparts an agreeable tang to the filling. The Georgians use dried cornelian cherries for this dish, but I have found that our domestic dried cherries work very well.

SERVES 4

> ¾ cup uncooked rice
> 1¼ cups water
> 1 teaspoon salt
> ½ cup tart dried cherries
> 3 medium onions, peeled and finely chopped
> 1 large garlic clove, peeled and minced
> 5 tablespoons butter
> ¼ cup chopped parsley
> Salt
> Freshly ground black pepper
> One 6- to 7-pound roasting hen
> Chopped parsley and dill, for garnish

Cook the rice with the water and salt until tender but firm, about 12 minutes. Set aside to cool. Meanwhile, soak the dried cherries in warm water to cover until soft. Drain and chop coarsely.

In a skillet sauté the onions and garlic in 4 tablespoons of the butter until golden. Stir in the cooked rice, the chopped cherries, and the parsley. Season to taste with salt and pepper.

Stuff the chicken with this mixture and sew it up. Rub the chicken all over with the remaining tablespoon butter, and place on a spit over a wood fire. The skin will crisp in no time; the chicken is done when the leg joint can be easily moved.

To serve, cool slightly, then cut into quarters. Garnish with chopped parsley and dill.

N O T E : The chicken may be roasted in a 350° F. oven for 2 hours.

# CHICKEN SALAD
## (Katmis Mkhali)

A newfangled way to serve chicken comes from my friend Marina Abesadze, a Tbilisi physician who is always experimenting in the kitchen, seeking to expand the repertoire of Georgian dishes while retaining traditional flavors. Marina makes *katmis mkhali* or Georgian chicken salad, a takeoff on the traditional *mkhali* or vegetable purée. Mixed at the last minute with shredded lettuce and pomegranate seeds, this *mkhali* is stunning. In true Georgian style, Marina serves the salad as one of many foods on the table. I like to offer it alone for lunch.

SERVES 8

> One 5- to 6-pound roasting chicken
> ¾ pound shelled walnuts
> 2 tablespoons ground coriander seed
> 2 teaspoons ground marigold
> 2 garlic cloves, peeled and crushed
> 2½ teaspoons salt, or to taste
> 5 tablespoons red wine vinegar
> 1½ to 2 cups chicken broth
> 4 scallions, including the green, minced
> 1 cup minced cilantro
> ½ cup minced fresh dill
> ½ cup minced celery leaves
> 2 cups loosely packed chiffonade of lettuce
> ½ cup pomegranate seeds

Place the chicken in a large pot with 1 quart cold water and bring to a boil. Simmer, covered, until tender, about 2 hours. Allow the chicken to cool in the broth.

Meanwhile, finely grind the walnuts, then mix them with the ground coriander, marigold, garlic, salt, and vinegar.

When the chicken has cooled, shred it fine. Using your hands, work in the seasoned nuts and enough chicken broth to bind. The texture of the salad should be almost a paste. Mix in the scallions, cilantro, dill, and celery, and chill for 3 to 5 hours.

One-half hour before serving, remove the salad from the refrigerator and allow to come to room temperature. Just before serving, stir in the lettuce and the pomegranate seeds.

# CHICKEN GIBLETS
# WITH WALNUTS
## (Kuchmachi)

*Kuchmachi,* a piquant combination of chicken gizzards and hearts, is like chunky chopped chicken liver with a Georgian twist. Believing that no part of an animal should go to waste, the Georgians use offal extensively. In addition to the more familiar liver and tongue, they enjoy hearts, lungs, and spleen, and often make *kuchmachi* from pork innards, particularly in the winter after the December slaughter. But the dish tastes just as flavorsome with the chicken parts more readily available in American stores.

**SERVES 8**

> ¾ pound mixed chicken gizzards and hearts (some liver may be included, too)
> 2 tablespoons butter
> ¾ cup shelled walnuts
> 1 small garlic clove, peeled and roughly chopped
> ¼ teaspoon dried summer savory
> ¼ teaspoon salt
> Dash cayenne
> 4 teaspoons red wine vinegar
> 3 tablespoons pomegranate seeds

Boil the gizzards and hearts in salted water until tender, about 1 hour, then drain. In a frying pan melt the butter and fry the giblets until lightly browned. Coarsely grind.

In a food processor, finely grind the walnuts.

In a mortar with a pestle, crush the garlic with the savory, salt, and cayenne. Stir into the minced giblets. Add the ground walnuts, vinegar, and pomegranate seeds, mixing well.

Serve at room temperature.

# DAREDZHAN'S
# DUCK CHAKHOKHBILI
# WITH WALNUTS
## (Ikhvis Chakhokhbili)

**M**y friend Daredzhan Abesadze claims that the best *chakhokhbili* is made with duck instead of chicken, and true to her native Kutaisi, she adds walnuts to her stew. Her duck *chakhokhbili* is a subtle presentation, a dish that improves upon standing.

SERVES 4

> One 5-pound duck, cut into 12 pieces
> 1 large onion, peeled and chopped
> 6 medium-sized ripe tomatoes, chopped
> 1 cup shelled walnuts, ground
> 1 tablespoon cornmeal
> 1 tablespoon flour
> 2 large garlic cloves, peeled
> ½ teaspoon ground coriander seed
> ½ teaspoon ground marigold
> ½ teaspoon salt
> Freshly ground black pepper
> ½ cup minced cilantro
> 2 tablespoons red wine vinegar

Preheat the oven to 350° F.

Place the pieces of duck in an ovenproof casserole, cover, and braise for 1 hour. Remove the duck and drain all the fat from the dish. Return the pieces of duck to the casserole and add the chopped onion. Cover and roast in the oven for 30 minutes more. Next layer on the chopped tomatoes and braise, covered, for an additional 30 minutes.

In a separate bowl mix together the remaining ingredients. Remove the casserole from the oven and transfer the duck and vegetables to a bowl. Cover to keep warm. Stir 1½ cups of the cooking liquid into the nut mixture to make a sauce. Return the duck and vegetables to the casserole and pour the sauce over, mixing well. Return the dish to the oven and bake for 10 minutes more. This *chakhokhbili* tastes even better reheated the second day.

# BRAISED PHEASANT
## (Moshushuli Khokhobi)

Georgians sometimes use brewed tea in cooking to impart flavor to dishes both savory and sweet. Although such recipes are not traditional, they are exotic and appealing to the Western palate. The following recipe takes advantage of several local foods in addition to tea: the pheasant native to the Rioni River valley, tangerines, hazelnuts, and wine. The method of slow-cooking ensures that the birds will be moist.

SERVES 4

¼ cup hazelnuts
1 heaping teaspoon black tea leaves
¼ cup boiling water
2 pheasants, cleaned and dressed, about 2½ pounds each
Salt
Freshly ground black pepper
2 tablespoons butter, softened
1 tangerine, peeled and separated into segments
2 tablespoons sweet red wine
2 tablespoons unsweetened grape juice

FOR GARNISH
Tangerine segments
Toasted hazelnuts
Red and white grapes

Preheat the oven to 350° F.

Toast the hazelnuts for 10 minutes until lightly browned, then rub off their skins between the edges of a tea towel. Grind them in a food processor.

Pour the boiling water over the tea leaves and let steep for 15 minutes.

Rinse the pheasants and pat them dry. Rub inside and out with salt and pepper, then rub with the butter. Grease a casserole just large enough to hold the pheasants and place them in it breast side up. Surround with segments from 1 tangerine.

Strain the tea. Stir in the wine, grape juice, and ground nuts. Pour this mixture over the pheasants, making sure some nuts remain on top

*(Continued)*

of the birds. Cover the casserole and bake for 1 hour, basting occasionally. Remove the cover and cook for 10 minutes more to brown.

Remove the pheasants from the sauce and serve garnished with tangerine segments, toasted hazelnuts, and red and white grapes.

VARIATION

If pheasant is unavailable, cornish hens may be substituted. Simply bake them for 1 hour and 15 minutes, plus 10 minutes to brown.

See also *Makvali* (page 123) for a blackberry sauce to serve with roast chicken.

# FISH

**G**eorgians particularly enjoy freshwater fish, such as *tsotskhali*. The name of this tiny, troutlike fish means "alive." In the past, revelers would arrive at a feast bearing live fish. As they entered the dining room they threw the squirming fish right onto the table as a mark of abundance and a celebration of life. The *tsotskhali* were quickly gathered up and whisked into the kitchen to be boiled for only a few minutes and returned to the table, absolutely fresh and unadorned. With other kinds of fish, Georgians serve piquant sauces. Poached flatfish from the Black Sea is usually enhanced with a fruit or walnut sauce, while sturgeon from the Caspian is often marinated and grilled.

## GRILLED TROUT WITH TARRAGON
### (Shemtsvari Kalmakhi)

**T**rout, along with the *khramuli* or barb of the carp family, are the favored freshwater fish in Georgia. Tbilisians enjoy taking raft picnics on the Kura River, stopping to fish for the excellent trout, which they eat on the spot after plunging it into boiling river water. Sometimes the fish is wrapped in walnut leaves and baked in a *ketsi*. The leaves keep the fish from charring and impart a delicate flavor. My favorite picnic fish is trout grilled with tarragon, a felicitous union of water and earth.

*(Continued)*

PROPORTIONS PER PERSON
   1 trout, cleaned and slit down the belly
   Salt
   Freshly ground black pepper
   1 tablespoon minced scallion
   4 or 5 thin slices lemon
   1 large sprig fresh tarragon
   Minced fresh tarragon for garnish

Prepare a charcoal fire.
   Lightly salt and pepper the insides of the trout. In the cavity place the scallion, lemon slices, and sprig of tarragon.
   Rub the skin of the trout with oil to keep it from sticking to the grill, then cook the fish over a hot fire for 5 minutes on each side.
   Serve garnished with tarragon.

Fisherman in a Red Shirt

# GRILLED MARINATED FISH
## (Tatris Basturma)

Georgians make this *basturma* with sturgeon from the Caspian Sea, but salmon (steak or fillet) and swordfish work equally well.

SERVES 4

  1 large onion, peeled and grated
  1 teaspoon salt
  Freshly ground black pepper
  1 large bay leaf, crushed
  1 large lemon, thinly sliced
  ¼ cup vegetable oil
  2 pounds sturgeon, cut into 2-inch chunks
  Minced scallion
  Lemon wedges

In a large bowl, mix together the onion, salt, pepper, bay leaf, lemon slices, and vegetable oil. Stir in the chunks of fish, tossing to coat them well. Cover and marinate in the refrigerator for 4 to 6 hours, or overnight.

Prepare a charcoal fire. Thread the fish onto skewers. When the coals are ready, grill the fish until just flaky. Serve immediately, garnished with minced scallion and lemon wedges.

# FISH WITH POMEGRANATE AND WALNUT SAUCE
## (Tevzi Brotseulis Tsvenshi)

This excellent cold fish will have your guests guessing at the ingredients. I like to use red snapper, even though it is not Georgian; its firm flesh and succulent taste hold their own against the rich nut sauce.

SERVES 3 TO 4

> 1 large fillet of whitefish, red snapper, or other firm fish
>     (1¼ pounds)
> Salt
> Freshly ground black pepper
> 2 tablespoons white flour
> 3 tablespoons vegetable oil
> 2 medium onions, peeled and chopped
> 1 tablespoon butter
> ½ cup shelled walnuts
> 1 large garlic clove, peeled
> 1 tablespoon minced hot red or green pepper
> ½ cup water
> ½ cup unsweetened pomegranate juice (available at health food
>     stores)
> 2 tablespoons tomato paste

Sprinkle the fish with salt and pepper. Dust both sides with flour. In a large skillet, heat the oil. Fry the fish, turning once, for 10 to 20 minutes, depending on the thickness of the fillet, until it is crusty and brown.

Meanwhile, sauté the onion in the butter over medium heat until golden, about 10 minutes.

Transfer the fish to a shallow flameproof casserole. Strew the cooked onions over it.

To make the sauce, grind the walnuts with the garlic and ½ teaspoon salt. Stir in the hot pepper, water, pomegranate juice, and tomato paste, mixing well.

Pour the sauce over the fish and bring to a boil. Simmer, covered, for 2 minutes. Remove from the heat and allow to cool, then refrigerate. Serve well chilled.

# COLD FISH IN
# CILANTRO SAUCE
### (Tevzi Kindzmarshi)

Here is a perfect summertime dish, cool and refreshing.

SERVES 3 TO 4

> 1 pound fillet of flounder
> Salt
> Freshly ground black pepper
> 1 bay leaf
> 1 cup water
> 1 small onion, peeled and chopped
> 6 tablespoons white wine vinegar
> ¾ cup minced cilantro

Season the fish with salt and pepper. Place in a skillet with the bay leaf and water. Top with the chopped onion. Bring to a boil. Reduce heat and poach, covered, for 8 to 10 minutes, until the fish is flaky. Transfer the fish and onion to a deep serving dish, reserving the broth. Cut the fish into strips.

In a bowl mix the vinegar with ½ cup of the reserved fish broth. Stir in the cilantro. Pour over the fish, cover the bowl, and refrigerate. Serve well chilled.

# SALMON IN
# VINEGAR SAUCE
## (*Uraguli Dzmarshi*)

The taste of salmon pairs well with vinegar in this appealing, sweet-sour dish.

SERVES 3 TO 4

> 1½ pounds salmon fillet
> Freshly ground black pepper
> 2 large bay leaves, crushed
> 1 medium onion, peeled and minced
> 1 cup white wine vinegar
> ½ cup water
> ½ teaspoon salt
> 2 tablespoons chopped parsley

Rub the salmon with pepper to taste and bay leaves. Let sit for 30 minutes.

Prepare a charcoal fire.

In a large skillet, simmer the onion with the vinegar, water, and salt for 15 minutes.

When the coals are ready, grill the salmon until just flaky. Transfer the fish to the skillet and heat gently in the sauce for a minute or two. Serve hot, garnished with parsley.

# SALMON BUGLAMA
## *(Tevzis Buglama)*

Similar to veal *buglama,* this salmon stew is full of delicious tomatoes and herbs. It is easy to prepare and very fresh-tasting. Serve with boiled potatoes or rice.

SERVES 4

> ¾ cup vegetable oil
> 2 pounds salmon, skinned and cut in 1½-inch pieces from thick
>   end of fillet or steak
> Salt
> Freshly ground black pepper
> 1 cup chopped cilantro
> 2 medium onions, peeled, sliced, and separated into rings
> 2 small lemons, sliced
> 4 bay leaves
> 1½ pounds (4 medium) ripe tomatoes, sliced

Pour ¼ cup of the oil into a deep saucepan large enough to hold the chunks of fish in a single layer, and swirl it to cover the bottom of the pan. Place the pieces of fish over the oil and season with salt and pepper. Top the fish with layers of cilantro, onions, lemons, and bay leaves, in that order. Pour another ¼ cup oil over the mixture, then lay on the sliced tomatoes. Add the remaining ¼ cup oil and more salt and pepper. Cover the pot and bring to a boil, reduce the heat to low, and simmer for 15 minutes, or until the fish is done.

# POACHED FISH
# WITH TOMATOES
## (Moshushuli Tevzi Pamidvrit)

A dish of perfect balance and simplicity.

SERVES 2

> 1 pound fillet of flounder or sole, cut into serving pieces
> Salt
> 1 medium onion, peeled, thinly sliced, and separated into rings
> ½ cup coarsely chopped fresh dill or cilantro
> 1 cup water
> 2 whole cloves
> 3 allspice berries
> 1 bay leaf
> 2 teaspoons vegetable oil
> 3 large ripe tomatoes, peeled and seeded (or substitute one
>     28-ounce can plum tomatoes, drained)
> ¼ teaspoon freshly ground black pepper
> ⅛ teaspoon cayenne (or less, to taste)
> 1 small garlic clove, peeled and minced
> Minced dill or cilantro

Season the fish with salt to taste and place in a pan. Strew the onion rings and herbs over it. Add the water, cloves, allspice, and bay leaf. Bring to a boil and poach, covered, until the fish is done, about 10 minutes.

Meanwhile, heat the oil in a skillet and fry the tomatoes over medium heat with the pepper, cayenne, garlic, and ½ teaspoon salt, breaking up the tomatoes with a fork. Cook until thickened, 7 or 8 minutes.

Remove the poached fish to a serving platter, along with the onions and herbs. Spoon the tomato sauce over the fish and serve, garnished with minced dill or cilantro.

# SAUCES

**G**rilled meats and fish are rarely served plain, since they make such excellent foils for sauce. Georgian sauces offer tremendous variety. Most are prepared from the same fruits, vegetables, and nuts that appear in various guises in other dishes. Plums, blackberries, blackthorn, grapes, pomegranates, tomatoes, and cornelian cherries are all puréed for sauce, as are cilantro, beets, garlic, and spinach. Georgian sauces are characteristically tart; some are piquant as well. An interesting feature of the Georgian sauce repertoire is that the same basic dressing adorns vastly different foods. Thus the nut sauce *satsivi* is served with meat, poultry, fish, and vegetables alike. Some sauces are so delicious in and of themselves that a common expression goes, "With a Georgian sauce you can swallow nails!" These sauces are rich enough to be served alone, accompanied only by a slice of bread for mopping.

## PLUM SAUCE
### *(Tkemali)*

*Tkemali* is the universal condiment in Georgia, used much as Americans use ketchup. It is prepared from the small, tart *tkemali* plum for immediate enjoyment or longterm keeping. *Tkemali* is meant to provoke the palate. It enlivens chicken and vegetables—such as the famous *lobio tkemali,* kidney beans in red plum sauce—and is the classic accompaniment to grilled lamb or beef. *Tkemali* also lends a distinctive flavor to soups and stews.

To make *tkemali* in America, I recommend using Santa Rosa plums. The finished sauce takes on a luscious shade of pink.

*(Continued)*

   1½ pounds plums (not too sweet or ripe)
   ¼ cup water
   ¾ teaspoon whole coriander seed
   1 teaspoon fennel seed
   2 large garlic cloves, peeled and roughly chopped
   1 teaspoon cayenne
   ½ teaspoon salt
   1 tablespoon finely minced fresh mint
   ⅓ cup finely minced cilantro

Cut the plums in half and remove the pits. Place in a saucepan with the water and bring to a boil. Simmer, covered, for 15 minutes, or until soft.

In a mortar with a pestle, pound together the coriander seed, fennel seed, garlic, cayenne, and salt to make a fine paste.

When the plums are soft, put them through a food mill and return to a clean pan. Bring to a boil and cook over medium heat, stirring, for 3 minutes. Stir in the ground spices and continue cooking until the mixture thickens slightly, another 5 minutes or so. Stir in the minced mint and cilantro and remove from the heat. Pour into a jar while still hot. Either cool to room temperature and keep in the refrigerator, or seal the jar for longer storage.

# CILANTRO SAUCE
## (Kindzis Satsebela)

Here is an excellent sauce to serve with grilled meat or chicken. It also complements vegetables nicely. Cilantro Sauce may be stirred into *lobio* or potato salad, or poured over cooked eggplant slices. This sauce tastes best after it has sat for 1 or 2 hours for the flavors to blend. (Cilantro is sometimes sold as fresh coriander or Chinese parsley.)

MAKES 2 CUPS

> 2 ounces apricot fruit leather
> ¼ cup boiling water
> ½ cup shelled walnuts
> 4 garlic cloves, peeled
> 1½ cups finely chopped cilantro
> 1½ cups finely chopped mixed parsley, dill, basil, tarragon
> ½ cup finely chopped scallions (including green part)
> ¼ cup freshly squeezed lemon juice
> 1½ teaspoons salt
> Freshly ground black pepper
> Dash cayenne
> 1 cup walnut oil

Soak the apricot leather in the boiling water until soft; stir until a purée is formed.

Grind the walnuts and the garlic together in a food processor, being careful not to grind them to a sticky paste. Next, add the apricot purée, the herbs, scallions, lemon juice, salt, pepper, and cayenne, and blend together. In a slow, steady stream, while the motor is running, add the walnut oil to form a thick sauce.

Allow to rest at room temperature for a couple of hours before serving. This sauce will keep, tightly covered and refrigerated, for several days. Bring to room temperature before using.

# T O M A T O    S A U C E
## (*P a m i d v r i s    S a t s e b e l a*)

This sauce often accompanies *basturma,* grilled marinated meat. The prunes add a hint of sweetness, while the coriander adds depth. Try serving this exciting tomato sauce with American-style steak.

MAKES 1 QUART

> 1 large onion, peeled and finely chopped
> 2 large garlic cloves, peeled and minced
> ¼ cup corn oil
> 3 pounds ripe tomatoes, cut into eighths
> ½ cup pitted prunes
> 1 teaspoon salt
> 1½ teaspoons freshly ground black pepper
> 2 teaspoons paprika
> 2¼ teaspoons ground coriander seed
> ½ teaspoon cayenne

In a saucepan sauté the onion and garlic in the oil until soft, then add the tomatoes. Cook gently, covered, for 45 minutes, or until the tomatoes are soft. Put through a food mill or strainer, pressing hard on the solids.

Return the sauce to the pan and add the remaining ingredients. Simmer, covered, for 10 minutes.

Serve hot or at room temperature. The sauce will keep in the refrigerator for up to a week. Reheat to serve.

# G A R L I C    S A U C E
## (*N i o r t s k a l i*)

A zestful companion to chicken *tabaka.*

MAKES ABOUT ½ CUP

> ½ cup chicken broth
> 3 or 4 garlic cloves, peeled and roughly chopped
> ¼ teaspoon salt

⅛ teaspoon paprika
Dash cayenne
1 tablespoon chopped cilantro

In a small saucepan heat the chicken broth. With a mortar and pestle, mash the garlic with the salt until a creamy paste is formed. Whisk the garlic into the chicken broth along with the paprika and cayenne. Just before serving, stir in the cilantro.

# BLACKBERRY SAUCE
## (Makvali)

This tart summer sauce refreshingly highlights roast chicken. Blackberries can be puréed, without cooking, into a thick sauce that looks like liquid ruby when spooned over the chicken. To give the sauce a lilt, Georgian cooks add unripe sour grapes to the sieved berries, but here I've substituted more readily available lemon juice.

MAKES ABOUT 1 CUP

1½ cups ripe blackberries
1 small garlic clove, peeled and roughly chopped
¼ teaspoon salt
½ small hot red or green pepper, minced
¼ cup minced mixed fresh dill and cilantro
1 or 2 teaspoons lemon juice

Force the blackberries through a fine sieve or food mill into a bowl. With a mortar and pestle, pound the garlic, salt, and hot pepper into a paste and add to the sieved blackberries. Stir in the minced herbs and lemon juice to taste. Serve at room temperature.

For two classic Georgian nut sauces, see *Satsivi* (page 97) and *Bazhe* (page 100).

# CHEESE, EGG, AND YOGURT DISHES

With its lush pastures, Georgia produces excellent dairy products. The milk from cows, sheep, goats, and water buffalo yields pungent cheeses and creamy yogurt, as well as a variety of other products, such as *nadugi,* a whey cheese that is often mixed with fresh herbs. Georgian cheeses are so nourishing and rich that in the western provinces of Guria, Samegrelo, and Imereti they traditionally took the place of butter.

Georgians like to mix different dairy products together in a single dish. *Nadugi,* for instance, is spread on thin slices of *suluguni* cheese, which are rolled into cornets for a tasty snack; *suluguni* is also frequently boiled in milk, then kneaded with mint. Other preparations are less elaborate. A simple treat enjoyed in Abkhazia is *akhshtsa,* or fresh hot goat's milk, for which a flat river stone is heated over coals and placed in the bottom of a wooden mug. The goat is then milked directly into the mug. As the milk hits the hot stone, it hisses, sending up steam and a marvelous aroma.

In addition to featuring recipes for strictly dairy dishes, this chapter includes vegetable dishes in which cheese, yogurt, or eggs predominate.

# COOKED CHEESE
# WITH MINT
## (Gadazelili Khveli)

One of my favorite Georgian foods is *gadazelili khveli,* warm *suluguni* cheese flavored with fresh mint. *Gadazelili khveli* is a fixture of the Georgian feast, usually presented straight from the kitchen near the beginning of the meal. Some cooks add twice as much milk as in the recipe below, serving the *gadazelili khveli* as a soup, but I like it best when the cheese is ascendant. To serve, the soft cheese is cut into portions and lifted from the milky broth. Here, whole-milk mozzarella substitutes well for the *suluguni.*

SERVES 6

   1 cup whole milk
   1 pound mozzarella, cut into chunks
   ½ teaspoon salt
   2 tablespoons chopped fresh mint

In a saucepan, bring the milk to a boil. Add the cheese and stir for about 2 minutes, until the cheese melts. With a slotted spoon transfer the cheese to a plate, keeping the milk at a simmer. Work the salt into the cheese with a wooden spoon. To mix in the mint, fold the cheese mass over and over until the mint is evenly distributed. Form the cheese into one large ball (or several smaller ones) and return it to the simmering milk. Heat gently a few minutes more, then turn out the cheese and the milk together into a bowl. Serve warm or at room temperature.

# GRILLED CHEESE
## (Shemtsvari Khveli)

In order for this recipe to work, the consistency of the cheese must be just right. Georgians usually grill *suluguni;* here I recommend using either fresh mozzarella or a semihard cheese like kasseri or salted ricotta. Supermarket mozzarella cannot be successfully grilled. Whether cooked in a skillet or over an open flame, this cheese is delicious—crusty and brown on the outside, creamy within.

SERVES 4

> 1 pound fresh mozzarella, or a favorite semihard cheese
> ½ cup olive oil
> Fresh mint or tarragon

Cut the cheese into ½-inch-thick sticks that are 3 inches long and 1 inch wide.

Heat the oil in a 10-inch cast-iron skillet. Add the cheese sticks. Cook, covered, over medium high heat, for 2 minutes, until golden. Turn the sticks and cook them, uncovered, for 1 minute more. With a slotted spatula, remove the cheese from the skillet and serve immediately, garnished with finely chopped fresh mint or tarragon.

To grill the cheese over an open flame, securely impale the whole round of cheese on a long, broad skewer. Rotate the cheese over the flame until golden on all sides. Serve immediately garnished with chopped fresh herbs.


# SKEWERED EGGS
## (Kerkshi Shemtsvari Kvertskhi)

Much more interesting than hard-boiled eggs, these eggs are perfect picnic fare, infused with a smoky taste from the fire.

Prepare a charcoal fire.

Place the tips of metal skewers in the hot coals until heated through. With the hot skewers, carefully pierce the shells of raw eggs lengthwise, one egg to a skewer. Place the eggs over the coals and grill until firm, about 10 minutes (depending on the heat of the fire).

# GEORGIAN EGG SALAD
## (*Azelila*)

*Azelila* is a tasty departure from traditional egg salad. Its name comes from the Georgian verb "to mix." This version is piquant, in the Abkhazian style; the variation is more subtle.

SERVES 4

> 4 large eggs
> 1 tablespoon butter, softened
> ¼ cup shelled walnuts, ground
> 2 tablespoons minced fresh dill
> Pinch salt
> 1 tablespoon *adzhika* (page 181) or hot Mexican salsa

Hard-boil the eggs and allow them to cool; separate the yolks from the whites. Mash the yolks with the softened butter. Stir in the ground walnuts, dill, salt, and the *adzhika*. Turn out onto a serving plate and surround with the chopped egg whites. Serve at cool room temperature.

VARIATION

> For a creamier salad, do not separate the hard-boiled eggs. Mash the eggs with 3 tablespoons of softened butter, the ground walnuts, the dill, 2 tablespoons each of minced cilantro and scallion (white part only), and ⅛ teaspoon salt. Sprinkle 2 tablespoons pomegranate seeds on top of the salad for garnish.

# GEORGIAN OMELET
## (Erbokvertskhi)

The Georgian name for omelet reveals that this dish was originally made with clarified butter, or *erbo*. But an equally delicious result is achieved with regular salted butter. This omelet is gratifying at breakfast and supper alike.

SERVES 2

6 large eggs
¼ cup shelled walnuts, ground
¼ teaspoon salt
Freshly ground black pepper
2 tablespoons butter
Scant ¼ teaspoon ground cinnamon
1 tablespoon pomegranate seeds (optional)

Lightly beat the eggs and stir in the walnuts, salt, and pepper to taste.

In a large skillet, melt the butter. When it is hot, pour in the egg mixture. With a fork, push the outer, cooked edges of the egg toward the center, tipping the pan to allow the uncooked portion to flow into the cleared space. Continue this procedure until the omelet is cooked, about 3 or 4 minutes. Fold over the sides of the omelet and slide it out onto a platter. Sprinkle with cinnamon and garnish with pomegranate seeds, if desired. Serve at once.

# CAULIFLOWER WITH EGG
## (Chirbuli)

*Chirbuli,* a specialty of the Black Sea coast in western Georgia, is usually a potpourri of vegetables into which beaten eggs are stirred at the last minute. Sometimes it is prepared with a single vegetable to highlight a specific flavor, and that is how I like it best. The most memorable recipes call for generous amounts of butter in addition to the egg, resulting in a rich and filling dish. Be careful not to overcook the eggs at the end. They should remain moist so that the mixture does not toughen.

SERVES 4

> 1 small (1 pound) cauliflower, separated into florets
> 2 small onions, peeled and finely chopped
> 8 tablespoons (1 stick) butter
> ¼ cup minced parsley
> 2 tablespoons minced cilantro
> 2 large eggs, beaten
> Salt
> Freshly ground black pepper

Steam the cauliflower over boiling water for 10 minutes. Drain.

Meanwhile, in a large frying pan sauté the onions until golden in 4 tablespoons of the butter. Add the remaining butter and stir in the cauliflower, turning the florets to coat with the butter. Cook, covered, for 10 minutes more, until tender.

Stir in the parsley, cilantro, and eggs. Toss to coat, cooking only until the eggs are done. Season to taste.

# GREEN BEANS WITH EGG
## (Mtsvane Lobios Chirbuli)

This *chirbuli* recipe produces a rich supper dish, the scrambled egg studded generously with beans.

SERVES 4

2 sprigs basil
1 sprig tarragon
2 sprigs summer savory
1 sprig dill
1 sprig parsley
½ pound green beans
Water
1 small onion, peeled and minced
¼ teaspoon salt
6 tablespoons (¾ stick) butter, in pieces
1 egg, well beaten

Coarsely chop the herbs. Trim the beans and cut them into small pieces. Place the beans in a single layer in a skillet and add just enough water to half cover them. Bring the water to a boil and stir in the onion, salt, and chopped herbs. Cover the skillet and simmer, covered, until the beans are soft and the water has been absorbed, 10 to 15 minutes. Add the butter to the pan and over medium heat sauté the beans lightly, stirring, until the butter has melted. Then pour on the beaten egg, cover the skillet, and cook for 2 or 3 minutes, or just until the egg has set. Stir lightly and turn out into a bowl.

# FRESH HERB AND EGG SALAD
## (Salati)

This tangy salad offers a novel way to serve fresh herbs if you don't want to present them plain on a platter. The use of sour cream for dressing betrays a Russian influence.

FOR EVERY 2 SERVINGS

> 1 large egg
> 12 sprigs each fresh dill, parsley, opal or green basil, and cilantro
>   (or more, to taste)
> Sour cream
> Salt
> Freshly ground black pepper

Hard-boil the egg.

Chop the herbs together fairly finely and place in a large salad bowl. Coarsely chop the egg and add to the bowl.

Dress the salad with just enough sour cream to moisten. Add salt and freshly ground black pepper to taste.

N O T E : Other herbs, such as tarragon and mint, may also be added.

# HERBED POTATOES
## WITH EGGS
### (Kartopilis Kaurma)

Eggs are frequently added to vegetable dishes to make them heartier and more filling. One of the most delicious combinations is *kartopilis kaurma,* a hot dish of potatoes mixed with eggs and lightly flavored with cilantro, usually brought steaming to the table during the course of a feast. Most *kaurma*s are made of meat or offal. Their name is derived from the Arabic *qawurma,* which defines meat preserved in layers of fat in an earthenware container, then used as needed either plain or in stews. Georgian *kaurma*s call for fresh meat or vegetables, deferring to the original only in their generous dose of butterfat.

SERVES 6 TO 8

>   3 medium onions, finely chopped
>   4 tablespoons (½ stick) butter
>   1½ pounds boiling potatoes
>   1 cup water
>   ½ teaspoon salt
>   3 leafy sprigs cilantro, minced
>   2 eggs, well beaten

Place the onions in a 2-quart saucepan with the butter. Cover and cook over low heat until the onions have softened, 25 to 30 minutes. Do not let them brown. Peel the potatoes, chop them, and add to the pot along with the water, salt, and cilantro. Cover and cook over medium low heat until the potatoes are soft, about 20 minutes. Stir in the beaten eggs and cook a few minutes longer, until they have set. Serve immediately.

# EGGPLANT WITH CHEESE AND YOGURT
## (Badridzhani Khvelit da Matsvnit)

Here eggplant proves a worthy carrier for butter, cheese, egg, and yogurt. The cholesterol count is admittedly high, but what a wonderful way to indulge!

SERVES 4

¾ pound eggplant
Olive oil
¼ pound feta cheese, crumbled
1 hard-boiled egg, mashed
4 tablespoons (½ stick) butter, softened
¾ cup yogurt, beaten

Preheat the oven to 500° F. Trim the ends from the eggplant, cut them in half lengthwise, and scoop out the seeds. Place the eggplant in a greased baking dish and brush the cut surfaces with olive oil. Bake until half done, about 15 minutes.

Meanwhile, stir the cheese and the hard-boiled egg into the softened butter, mixing well.

Remove the eggplant from the oven and reduce the heat to 350° F. Stuff the cavities of the eggplant with the cheese mixture and return to the oven. Bake 45 minutes more.

Serve with a pitcher of beaten yogurt to pour over the eggplant.

# SPINACH WITH YOGURT
## (Ispanakhi Matsvnit)

Dairy products deepen not only the taste but also the texture of many vegetable dishes, adding an appealing creaminess. Yogurt is especially favored for this quality. Some years ago Madison Avenue decided to capitalize on the longevity of certain Georgians by claiming that their advanced age was due to a steady diet of yogurt. While Georgians do indeed consume vast amounts of yogurt, their long lives probably have more to do with attitude or joie de vivre than diet, despite Madison Avenue's claims. Regular consumption of this spinach with yogurt, however, should keep you both happy and healthy.

SERVES 4

> 1 pound spinach
> 2 leafy sprigs cilantro
> 1 garlic clove, peeled and roughly chopped
> Pinch salt
> 1 cup plain yogurt

Wash the spinach well and cook it, covered, for 5 minutes in the water clinging to the leaves. Drain thoroughly. With your hands, squeeze out any excess moisture, then mince.

Using a mortar and pestle, pound together the cilantro, garlic, and salt and add them to the yogurt. Beat the mixture well; stir in the spinach. Serve chilled.

See also Green Beans with Yogurt (page 153) and Cornmeal Pudding with Cheese (page 151).

# BREADS
# AND GRAINS

**B**read is an object of reverence in Georgia, where until recently most families were close enough to the land to appreciate the labors of growing, harvesting, threshing, and milling wheat. Many rituals grew up around the storage of grain and the preparation of bread. In highland households, wheat flour was kept in a special chest, which only the eldest woman in the family was allowed to open. As added precaution, a piece of charcoal was frequently buried in the flour to keep out the devil. So respected was bread that even the dough left in the kneading trough and on the baker's hands was meticulously scraped clean and formed into a small loaf that was handled with particular care.

Dozens of differently shaped loaves are still common to Georgia's various regions, where a wide variety is baked, from crisp, unleavened sheets to breads rich with butter and sugar. Most Georgian breads are baked in the *toné,* although certain kinds may be fried in a skillet or baked in a clay *ketsi* over an open flame.

Flours other than wheat are also milled in Georgia. In the western part of the republic, corn essentially replaces wheat; there *mchadi* or corncakes are eaten in place of wheat bread. In the mountainous regions, when wheat flour is scarce, the roots of wild plants are first dried and then ground for bread additives, creating a rather coarse, though tasty, loaf.

# GEORGIAN CHEESE BREAD I
## (Khachapuri)

No feast would seem proper without the marvelous cheese bread, *khachapuri*. *Khachapuri* is found throughout Georgia in many guises —round, rectangular, and boat-shaped. The dough can be yeasty with a thick crust, many-layered and flaky, or tender and cakelike. The bread is usually filled with a fresh, slightly sour cheese like *imeruli* (Imeretian) or *suluguni,* but salted cheeses like *bryndza* may also be used, as long as they are soaked first. The cheese is grated and mixed with eggs to bind, with butter added if it is not creamy enough. The filling is then either completely enclosed in dough or served in an open-faced pie.

If any equivalent to fast food exists in Georgia, it must be *khachapuri*. Although Georgians are not accustomed to eating out frequently, even the smallest towns have hole-in-the-wall cafés where piping hot *khachapuri* may be consumed on the spot or taken out. On Tbilisi's main thoroughfare a line often stretches up steep steps and out into the street from a cellar café specializing in *khachapuri*. The café is steamy from the heat of massive ovens where hundreds of breads are baked in short order every day. This café, like most, offers *khachapuri* made with a yeast dough, which provides a substantial meal. For those desiring extra sustenance, the *khachapuri* may be topped with a cracked egg and returned to the oven until the egg sizzles. My favorite version of this cholesterol-rich *khachapuri* is the *adzharuli khachapuri* or Adzharian cheese bread, found in Batumi on the Black Sea coast and appropriately boat-shaped.

At home, *khachapuri* is more often made without yeast, with baking soda (a European import) or yogurt used to tenderize the dough. After the cheese filling is enclosed, the bread is often cooked on top of the stove in a cast-iron skillet. Better yet, *khachapuri* may be baked over an open fire in a clay or stone *ketsi,* so that the fire imparts a slightly smoky taste to the bread.

This first version of *khachapuri* yields a rich, flaky cheese pastry.

2 cups unbleached white flour
½ teaspoon salt
12 tablespoons (1½ sticks) cold butter, cut in pieces
2 eggs
¼ cup plain yogurt
1¼ pounds mixed Muenster and Havarti cheeses
1 egg yolk, beaten

Put the flour and salt in a medium bowl and cut in the butter until the mixture resembles coarse cornmeal. Beat 1 egg and stir in the yogurt, then add to the flour mixture. Form into a ball and chill for 1 hour.

Grate the cheeses coarsely, beat the other egg, and stir it into the cheese. Set aside.

Preheat the oven to 350° F. Grease a large baking sheet. On a floured board roll the dough to a rectangle about 12 x 17 inches. Trim the edges. Spread the cheese mixture on half the dough and then fold the other half over to enclose it, sealing and crimping the edges.

Transfer the bread to the baking sheet and brush with beaten egg yolk. Bake for 50 minutes, or until browned. The bread is best served slightly warm, cut into small squares.

# GEORGIAN CHEESE BREAD II

This recipe is for a golden yeast bread. With its fanciful topknot, this *khachapuri* makes a stunning centerpiece for the feast table. Cut into wedges to serve.

SERVES 8 TO 12

3/4 cup milk
1½ packages (4½ teaspoons) active dry yeast
½ teaspoon honey
6 tablespoons (3/4 stick) butter, at room temperature
1/4 teaspoon ground coriander seed
1¾ teaspoons salt
2 cups unbleached white flour
1 pound Muenster cheese
½ pound pot cheese
3 eggs
1 tablespoon melted butter

Heat the milk to lukewarm (105° F.). Dissolve the yeast and honey in 1/4 cup of the milk. Set aside to proof for 10 minutes, then stir in the remaining milk. Add the room temperature butter, the ground coriander seed, 1½ teaspoons of the salt, and the flour, mixing well.

Turn the dough out onto a floured board and knead until smooth and elastic, about 10 minutes. Place in a greased bowl, turning the dough to grease the top. Cover and allow to rise in a warm place until doubled in bulk, 1½ to 2 hours.

To prepare the filling, grate the Muenster cheese. In a medium bowl, with a wooden spoon, cream the pot cheese. Stir in the grated Muenster until well blended. Beat the eggs and stir into the cheese mixture along with the remaining 1/4 teaspoon salt. Beat until smooth and light. Set aside.

When the dough has doubled in bulk, punch it down and then let rise again until doubled, about 45 minutes. Punch down and divide into 3 equal pieces.

On a floured board, roll each piece of dough into a circle about 12 inches in diameter. Grease three 8-inch cake or pie pans. Center a round of dough in each pan.

Divide the cheese mixture into 3 equal parts. Place ⅓ of the filling on each circle of dough, heaping it in the center. Then begin folding the edges of the dough in toward the center, moving in a clockwise direction, allowing each fold of dough to overlap the previous one, until the cheese mixture is completely enclosed in the pleated dough. Grasp the excess dough in the center of the bread and twist it into a topknot to seal.

Preheat the oven to 375° F.

Let the breads stand for 10 minutes, then brush with the melted butter. Bake for about 45 minutes, or until browned. Slip the *khachapuri* out of the pans and serve hot or at room temperature.

## FILLED BREADS

Each region of Georgia has a local variation on the much-loved cheese bread, *khachapuri*. Popular fillings include meat, vegetables, and herbs. In remote Racha province, the specialty is *lobiani*, named for its filling of mashed beans. Georgian Jews in Kutaisi prepare *kartopiliani*, bread stuffed with potatoes and onions. And in Tskhneti, on the outskirts of Tbilisi, I tasted *khachapuri tarkhunit*, bread generously filled with salted cheese and herbs.

The European-style dough I offer here provides a rich envelope for 3 different fillings. This dough is a specialty of Mzia Gachechiladze. Her name comes from the Georgian word for "sun," which perfectly suits her brightness.

*(Continued)*

# B E A N   B R E A D
## (*L o b i a n i*)

10 tablespoons (1¼ sticks) butter, softened
2 eggs
2 cups sour cream
4 cups unbleached white flour
1 teaspoon baking soda, divided into 4 parts

*FILLING*
1 pound dried kidney beans, soaked overnight in water to cover
3 or 4 medium onions, peeled
⅔ cup vegetable oil
1 teaspoon ground coriander seed
2 teaspoons salt
Freshly ground black pepper

1 egg yolk

Cream the butter. Beat in the eggs and sour cream. Mix in the flour to make a soft dough.

On a floured board roll the dough to a 15- x 18-inch rectangle. Sprinkle with ¼ teaspoon of the baking soda. Fold the dough in half, then in half again, and roll out once more to a 15- x 18-inch rectangle. Sprinkle with ¼ teaspoon of the remaining soda. Repeat the folding process. Perform the process 4 times, until all of the baking soda has been incorporated into the dough. After folding the dough the last time, place it in a floured bowl, cover it, and leave it to rise for 6 to 8 hours at room temperature or 2 to 3 hours in the sun, until doubled in bulk. (Don't let the dough sit for any longer or it will begin to sour.)

Meanwhile, make the filling. Drain the kidney beans and cover them with fresh water. Bring to a boil and simmer until soft, about 1 hour. Drain. Mash the beans until no lumps remain.

Dice the onions. Sauté them in the oil until soft. Stir the onions into the mashed beans and add the ground coriander seed, salt, and pepper to taste. Divide the bean mixture in half and set aside.

Preheat the oven to 350° F.

When the dough has risen, divide it into 2 parts. On a lightly floured baking sheet, roll 1 part of the dough into a 10- x 18-inch rectangle. Spread half the bean mixture over half of the dough and fold the other half over it to cover. Seal the bread by bringing the lower edges up over the top of the dough to form a rim. Make another bread with the remaining dough.

Brush the breads with beaten egg yolk and bake for 40 to 45 minutes, until nicely browned. Serve warm or at room temperature.

## POTATO BREAD
### (Kartopiliani)

Follow the directions for making baking-soda dough given in the previous recipe. Substitute the following mixture for the bean filling:

4 pounds potatoes
4 medium onions, peeled
¾ cup vegetable oil
1 tablespoon salt
1 teaspoon freshly ground black pepper

Boil the potatoes until soft. Peel and mash well. Dice the onions and sauté in the oil until soft. Stir them into the mashed potatoes along with the salt and pepper.

## CHEESE AND HERB BREAD
### (*Khachapuri Tarkhunit*)

Follow the directions given in the recipe for *Lobiani* for making baking-soda dough. Substitute the following mixture for the bean filling:

8 eggs
½ pound (2 sticks) butter, softened
½ pound farmer cheese
½ pound feta cheese
2 cups loosely packed fresh mint or tarragon
1 teaspoon salt
Freshly ground black pepper

Hard-boil the eggs. Cream the butter and add the mashed hard-boiled yolks, mixing well. Dice the whites and add to the egg mixture. Crumble the cheese and stir in. Finely chop the mint or tarragon and stir it in along with the salt and pepper to taste.

## BAKED NOODLES WITH CHEESE
### (*Achma-Makarina*)

Like its relative, *khachapuri*, *achma-makarina* is a show-stopper. The tender egg dough browns beautifully in the oven, the folds of the top layer reminiscent of so many valleys and dunes. The outer crust of the pie is crisp, the inner layers creamy. Although time-consuming, this noodle pie is both visually and gastronomically rewarding.

SERVES 10

2 cups unbleached white flour
1½ teaspoons salt
3 large eggs, beaten
¼ cup warm water
2 tablespoons salt
1 tablespoon olive oil
6 tablespoons (¾ stick) butter, melted

¾ pound mixed Havarti and Muenster cheeses, coarsely grated
   (6 cups)
¾ cup chopped parsley

To make the noodle dough, mix the flour and salt. Make a well in the center and pour in the eggs. Mix well. Add the water to make a soft dough. Knead for a few minutes. Place the dough in a clean bowl and cover with a damp towel. Allow to rest for 1 hour.

Divide the dough into 8 pieces. On a floured board, roll out each piece very thinly to a 9- x 12-inch rectangle. As each sheet of dough is prepared, place it on a well-floured piece of wax paper.

Grease a 9- x 13-inch baking pan.

Bring a large kettle of water to a boil with the salt and olive oil. Have ready a large bowl of ice water and a colander.

Preheat the oven to 400° F.

When the water boils, lower 1 sheet of dough into it, ladling water over the dough so that its surface is covered. Boil for 1 minute. (If, despite all precautions, the thin sheets of dough stick to the wax paper, don't panic. Simply place the dough, paper and all, in the water. Within a few seconds the paper will separate from the dough; remove it from the water and proceed with the cooking.)

With a large, flat strainer carefully remove the sheet of dough from the boiling water and immediately plunge it into the ice water. Transfer to a colander to drain. With your hands, gently squeeze any excess water from the dough.

Place the sheet of dough in the prepared pan and brush with melted butter. Repeat this process with 3 more sheets of dough.

After 4 sheets have been placed in the pan, sprinkle on the grated cheese and parsley. Top with the remaining 4 sheets of dough, each cooked as above and brushed with butter.

Bake in the preheated oven for 30 minutes, until browned.

N O T E : Another favorite cheese, such as feta, may be used instead of Muenster and Havarti for the filling.

# DUMPLINGS
## (*Khinkali*)

*Khinkali* are made with a variety of fillings. In the mountains the choice is usually ground lamb, since that is most readily available, but elsewhere the filling is more often a mixture of beef and pork. The dumplings may also be stuffed with cheese or greens. Although many villages claim their *khinkali* are best, due to the mineral waters from local hot springs, *khinkali* from the town of Pasanauri, north of Tbilisi, are generally acknowledged as superior.

One trick to making good *khinkali* is to mix the flour with warm water, which yields a more tender dough. Shaping the dumplings is important, too, and takes some skill. My first clumsy attempts at making what seemed like an impossible number of pleats were met with laughter by the virtuoso chef instructing me, but eventually I mastered the process. The idea is to make as many pleats as possible as you bunch the dough around the filling: Anything less than 20 is considered unprofessional.

*Khinkali* are served hot, with no garnish other than coarsely ground black pepper. And there is an art to eating them. The doughy topknot is never consumed, but used as a handle for holding the hot dumplings. With your fingers, pick up a dumpling by the topknot—never use a fork or the juice will escape onto the plate instead of into your mouth. Take a bite, catching the first stream of juice in your mouth. After eating the meaty part of the dumpling, leave the topknot on the plate, or else toss it to any eager dogs that might be about. (Pasanauri dogs are *khinkali* fanciers; they mill around the garden restaurants hoping for a treat.) Leftover *khinkali*, if any, needn't go to the dogs, however. They are excellent the next day, fried lightly in butter and served with yogurt for breakfast.

MAKES 25 DUMPLINGS

**4 cups unbleached white flour**
**1¼ teaspoons salt**
**1¼ cups warm water**

**1 pound mixed ground beef and pork (not too lean)**
**½ teaspoon freshly ground black pepper**
**1¼ teaspoons salt**

Pinch cayenne
¼ teaspoon ground caraway seed
3 small onions, peeled
½ cup warm water or beef bouillon

Combine the flour, salt, and warm water to make a firm dough. Knead for 5 minutes, then let sit, covered, for 30 to 40 minutes.

Meanwhile, make the filling. Mix the ground meats and spices. Grind the onions and stir them into the meat mixture. With your hands, knead in the water or bouillon.

Divide the dough into 25 pieces. On a floured board, roll each piece out to a 6-inch round. Place about 2 tablespoons of filling in the center of each round. Make accordion pleats all the way around the filling by folding the edges of the dough in toward the center. Move in a clockwise direction, allowing each fold of dough to overlap the previous one, until the filling is completely enclosed in the pleated dough. Holding the dumpling firmly in one hand, twist the pleats together at the center to seal, breaking off the excess dough at the topknot.

Cook the dumplings in salted, boiling water for 12 to 15 minutes. Serve hot.

VARIATION

For cheese *khinkali,* make the following filling:

1 pound farmer cheese
1 teaspoon salt
Freshly ground black pepper
2 eggs

Press the farmer cheese through a sieve into a bowl. Beat in the salt, pepper, and eggs, mixing well.

Proceed as directed above.

# SAGE AND MINT FRITTERS
## (Pyshki)

These aromatic fried breads are a specialty of the eastern Georgian highlands, where wild sage grows in abundance.

MAKES 2 DOZEN FRITTERS

½ package (1½ teaspoons) active dry yeast
1½ cups lukewarm water (105° F)
1 small onion, peeled and finely chopped
2 tablespoons butter
1 tablespoon minced fresh sage
1 tablespoon minced fresh mint
3 cups unbleached white flour
Vegetable oil for frying

In a large bowl, dissolve the yeast in ¼ cup of the lukewarm water. Cover and leave to proof for 10 minutes.

Meanwhile, sauté the chopped onion in the butter until golden. Set aside to cool slightly.

When the yeast is bubbly, slowly add the remaining lukewarm water (make sure the water is still 105° F). Stir in the minced herbs and enough flour to make a loose batter. Stir in the onions. Cover the batter and allow to rise for 1½ hours, until light but not quite doubled in bulk.

In a large skillet, heat 1 inch of vegetable oil. Drop the batter by generous tablespoonsful into the hot oil. (Do not use more batter or the fritters will be heavy.) Cook the fritters over high heat until puffed and brown, turning once.

# WALNUT BALLS
## (Khenagi)

*Khenagi* are a specialty of the Georgian Jews. Jews have inhabited the Caucasus region for centuries and are considered by some to be the descendants of the mysterious Khazars, who disappeared in the tenth century. Until the wave of emigration to Israel in the 1970s and 1980s, Tbilisi boasted a sizable Jewish population, with a lovely old synagogue not far from the downtown Georgian Orthodox cathedral. With its own bakery for Passover matzoh and a slaughteryard for supplying kosher chicken and meat, Tbilisi's synagogue was better maintained than most under Soviet rule.

The cuisine of the Georgian Jews is Georgian in spirit, although a few specialties, like *khenagi,* are distinctly their own. Similar to matzoh balls, *khenagi* use walnuts for binding instead of meal. They are surprisingly light and offer an unusual alternative to the traditional matzoh balls served in soup.

MAKES ABOUT 3 DOZEN DUMPLINGS

½ **pound shelled walnuts**
2 **eggs**

In a food processor grind the walnuts to a paste. Beat the eggs well, then stir in the ground walnuts.

Bring a large kettle of salted water to a boil.

Moisten your hands with water. With your fingers make 1-inch balls, using about 1 tablespoon of the walnut mixture for each.

Drop the nut balls into boiling water and simmer them, covered, for 15 minutes.

Serve in chicken or vegetable soup.

# SPICE BREAD
## (*Nazuki*)

Most Georgian breads do not reproduce well in a standard oven, relying as they do for both taste and texture on the intense heat of the *toné*. One exception is the enriched spice bread known as *nazuki*. Variations of *nazuki* are found throughout the Middle East, but the addition of ground coriander makes this version distinctively Georgian. While the Georgians do not eat *nazuki* toasted for breakfast with lemon marmalade, I love it that way.

MAKES 4 SMALL LOAVES

> ¼ cup milk
> 1 package (1 tablespoon) active dry yeast
> Pinch sugar
> 2 eggs, at room temperature, well beaten
> 8 tablespoons (1 stick) unsalted butter, melted and cooled
> ¼ cup sugar
> Generous ½ teaspoon salt
> 2 teaspoons ground cinnamon
> ¼ teaspoon ground cloves
> 1 teaspoon ground coriander seed
> 1 teaspoon vanilla extract
> 2½ cups unbleached white flour
>
> 1 egg yolk, beaten

Heat the milk to lukewarm (105° F.). Stir in the yeast and pinch of sugar. Leave to proof for 10 minutes, or until the mixture begins to foam. Stir in the eggs, melted butter, sugar, salt, spices, and vanilla extract. Add enough flour to make a soft dough.

Turn the dough out onto a floured board and knead until smooth and elastic, about 10 minutes. Place in a greased bowl, turning to grease the top. Cover and allow to rise until doubled in volume, 1½ to 2 hours.

Divide the dough into 4 pieces. Roll each piece out into a 6-inch oval about ½ inch thick. Place the loaves on a greased baking sheet and leave to rise, covered, for ½ hour.

Preheat the oven to 375° F.

With your thumb make indentations in the dough in decorative rows, then brush the loaves with beaten egg yolk. Bake for 15 to 20 minutes, until golden.

# C O R N C A K E S
## (Mchadi)

*Mchadi,* or corncakes, are meant to be baked in a *ketsi* over an open fire, which imparts a delicate flavor. They can also successfully be prepared in a cast-iron skillet, however. Because *mchadi* are dry, they are perfect for sopping up sauce from one of the flavorsome Georgian stews. And since they are bland, *mchadi* provide an excellent foil for the lavishly seasoned foods of the western Georgian table. If you serve these corncakes to complement a different sort of meal, try topping them while still hot with a slice of fresh mozzarella.

SERVES 6

> 1 cup stone-ground cornmeal (preferably white)
> ¼ teaspoon salt
> ¾ cup cold water

Mix all the ingredients together to make a sticky dough. Form into 6 oval patties.

Preheat a 10-inch cast-iron skillet. When the skillet is hot, place the cornmeal cakes in it. Cover and cook over low heat for 8 minutes; turn and cook for 8 to 10 minutes more. Serve hot.

N O T E : For success in making these western Georgian cornmeal specialties, look for stone-ground white cornmeal and grits. Yellow cornmeal is acceptable, but the texture will be wrong if it is not coarsely ground.

# CORNMEAL PUDDING
## (Gomi)

Although *gomi* was originally made with millet, these days it is prepared with cornmeal. Corn proved a more reliable crop than the indigenous millet the Georgians had grown for centuries. It also proved more palatable, if we are to believe the report of Sir John Chardin. Here is what he has to say about *gomi:*

> Their usual Grain is *Gom;* which is a sort of Grain as small as Coriander Seed, and very much resembles Millet. . . . It is insipid and heavy. Yet it is presently boyl'd, and in less than half an hour after it is put into the Water, they stir it softly with a stick; and after it has stood never so little upon the Fire, it turns into Past. When the Grain is all dissolv'd, and the Past well wrought together, they lessen the Fire, let the water boyl away, and the Past harden and dry in the skellet where it was boyl'd.
>
> This Past is very white; and some there is, which they make as white as Snow. They serve it upon little Woodden Peels made on purpose. And this sort of bread the Turks call Pasta, the Mingrelians, Gom, being easily brok'n between the Fingers: but it is of a very cold and laxative Quality; nor is it worth any thing, after it is once cold, or when it is heated a second time. . . . 'Tis all the Bread they have, nor have they any other; and indeed they are so accustom'd to it, that they prefer it before Bread made of Wheat, as I have observ'd in most parts of those Countries which I have seen. Nor do I wonder at it; for when Necessity constrain'd me to make it my Food, I found it so acceptable to my Palate, that I could hardly leave it, when I came where I met with our usual Bread. Besides, I found my self very well, and my Body in a better Condition of Health than before . . . but it requires good store of Wine to wash it down, to correct and temper its cold and laxative Quality. . . .

*Gomi* tastes similar to the more familiar Italian polenta or Rumanian *mamaliga,* with the difference that like the pudding Chardin tasted, it is pale white rather than yellow.

SERVES 4

   **1 cup grits (preferably white stone-ground)**
   **2 cups water**
   **Salt**

In a heavy saucepan cook the grits in salted water over low heat, covered, until they are thick and steaming.

## CORNMEAL PUDDING WITH CHEESE
### *(Elardzhi)*

A richer version of *gomi,* for cheese lovers.

SERVES 6

> 1 recipe *gomi* (opposite)
> ¾ pound mozzarella, cut into pieces

Stir the cheese into the cooked *gomi* until it melts. (It will be stringy.) Serve piping hot.

**Three Princes Carousing on the Grass**

# VEGETABLES

**E**very Georgian meal features vegetables, both raw and cooked, and together with bread they form the foundation of Georgian cuisine. Folk wisdom calls for "onions, bread, and a kind heart" —nothing more is needed in life. One reason for the popularity of vegetables is their abundance; another reflects the religious proscriptions of the Georgian Orthodox Church. The church calendar set a strict regimen of fasts and feasts, and for religious Georgians in the past, nearly six months of the year represented days when they were expected to abstain from meat, eggs, and dairy products. Never ones to eat poorly, the Georgians devised delicious ways with the foods they were allowed to consume—vegetables and grains. Even on those days when meat and dairy products were permitted, more often than not Georgians cooked them with their favorite vegetables. For several centuries now Georgians have enjoyed such vegetables typical of the Mediterranean kitchen as eggplant and spinach, along with such new-world crops as green beans, potatoes, and peppers.

In vegetable cookery, as in the repertory of Georgian sauces, a few basic preparations are applied to many different products. Thus there are numerous types of *mkhalis*, or vegetable purées, and *boranis*, boiled vegetables with yogurt. These dishes are never redundant, however, since each vegetable lends a distinct taste and texture to the final dish. Georgian vegetables are fabulous, so delicious that even the most dedicated meat-eater may soon find himself a convert.

# GREEN BEANS WITH YOGURT
## (Mtsvane Lobios Borani)

*B*orani refers to a dish of boiled vegetables to which yogurt is added; an elaborate version calls for the addition of fried chicken as well. Georgian *borani* is similar to the Persian *borani-e* or Indian *boorani*, all legacies of Mongol influence. For a dramatic presentation, serve this green bean *borani* with chicken *tabaka*.

SERVES 4 TO 6

- 1 pound green beans, trimmed
- 1 onion, peeled and minced
- 6 tablespoons (¾ stick) butter
- ¼ teaspoon cinnamon
- Pinch ground cloves
- Freshly ground black pepper
- 1 small garlic clove, peeled and roughly chopped
- ½ teaspoon salt
- 1 cup plain yogurt
- ¼ cup ice water
- ½ cup chopped mixed fresh herbs (basil, tarragon, cilantro, parsley, dill, summer savory)
- 1 tablespoon chopped fresh mint (optional)

Parboil the beans for 4 to 5 minutes, until crisp-tender. Meanwhile, in a large frying pan sauté the onion in 4 tablespoons butter until soft.

Drain the beans and chop coarsely (each bean should be in 2 to 3 pieces). Add the beans to the onion along with the remaining 2 tablespoons butter. Stir in the cinnamon, cloves, and pepper. Cook, covered, for 10 to 15 minutes, until the beans are very soft.

In a mortar with a pestle, pound the garlic with the salt to a paste. Whip the yogurt with the ice water and add it to the pounded garlic.

Stir the fresh herbs into the beans and cook for 1 minute more, then turn out onto a plate. Pour the yogurt over the beans and garnish with fresh mint, if desired.

VARIATION

If green beans are not in season, substitute 2 pounds of cooked spinach from which all excess moisture has been squeezed.

# GREEN BEAN PURÉE
## (Mtsvane Lobios Mkhali)

Among the most popular vegetables in Georgia are green beans, or *lobio,* which are prepared in many different ways—with butter and eggs, with nuts, with tomatoes, with plum sauce. Green beans are best picked while young and fresh, but older, stringier beans can still add good flavor to stews and purées, as in this pleasing side dish.

SERVES 4 TO 6

  1 pound green beans
  ½ cup shelled walnuts
  3 garlic cloves, peeled
  ½ cup chopped cilantro
  ½ cup chopped parsley
  1 tablespoon chopped fresh dill
  1 tablespoon red wine vinegar

Trim the beans and cook them in boiling water until very soft. Drain.

Grind the walnuts in a food processor. Briefly process them with the garlic and herbs. Add the beans and process to make a purée. Stir in the vinegar and cool to room temperature before serving.

N O T E : For variations on this purée, see the recipe for Beet Purée (page 160).

# GREEN BEAN SALAD
## (Mtsvane Lobios Salati)

The dressing for this simple salad is similar to a French vinaigrette, though zestier. Use very fresh, tender beans.

SERVES 4

  1 pound young green beans
  1 large garlic clove, peeled and minced
  ½ cup chopped cilantro
  3 tablespoons olive oil
  2 tablespoons red wine vinegar

Trim the beans and cook them in boiling salted water until just tender, about 8 minutes. Drain well and mix with the remaining ingredients. Chill for several hours, but bring to near room temperature before serving.

# KIDNEY BEAN SALAD
## (*Lobio*)

The word *lobio* also designates dried beans and the salads prepared from them, mainstays of the Georgian table. Fine red and white kidney beans, smaller than our domestic varieties, grow wild in Georgia and are sold at the market, dried but not sterilized. Sometimes bugs hide in these beans. While American processing has taken care of aesthetics, too often our beans have languished on supermarket shelves. Try to find small beans that are not old and starchy.

*Lobio* is made in dozens of different ways: moistened with herb vinaigrette, puréed with tangy plum sauce, seasoned simply with butter and eggs, or mixed with lettuce and celery. In the recipe that follows, the predominant flavoring comes from walnuts. This russet salad is nicely set off by the earthy golds and greens of other Georgian foods.

SERVES 6 TO 8

½ pound small kidney beans
¾ teaspoon salt
1 small onion, peeled and finely chopped
2 sprigs cilantro
1 sprig parsley
½ cup walnuts
1 garlic clove, peeled
1 small hot pepper (about 1 inch long)
¼ teaspoon cinnamon
Pinch ground cloves
½ teaspoon ground marigold
½ to ¾ cup pomegranate juice
Pomegranate seeds

Soak the beans overnight in water to cover. The next day, drain and rinse them. Place in a large pot and cover with fresh water. Add ½ teaspoon of the salt. Bring the water to a boil and simmer until the beans are tender, about 1 hour. Drain. While the beans are still warm, stir in the chopped onion.

Grind the cilantro and parsley together with the walnuts, garlic, and hot pepper. Add to the beans.

In a small cup mix together the cinnamon, cloves, remaining ¼ teaspoon salt, and the marigold; stir into the bean mixture. Pour in enough pomegranate juice to moisten the beans and mix well.

Allow the beans to cool to room temperature, then serve liberally garnished with pomegranate seeds.

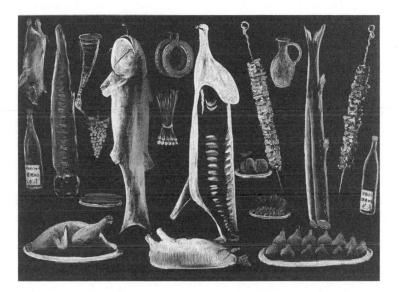

Still Life

# KIDNEY BEANS WITH PLUM SAUCE
## (Lobio Tkemali)

This is the classic recipe for *lobio,* simple to prepare if *tkemali* is on hand. If not, the variation at the end of the recipe offers an American version that calls for ingredients likely to be in the pantry.

SERVES 6

>½ pound dried kidney beans
>½ teaspoon salt
>½ cup *tkemali* (page 119)
>Salt
>Freshly ground black pepper
>Cilantro

Soak the beans overnight in water to cover. The next day, drain and rinse them. Place in a large pot and cover with fresh water. Add ½ teaspoon salt. Bring the water to a boil and simmer until the beans are tender, about 1 hour. Drain. While the beans are still warm, mash them. Stir in the *tkemali* and season with salt and pepper to taste. Serve at room temperature, garnished with cilantro.

VARIATION

>1 cup dried kidney beans
>2 garlic cloves, peeled, 1 cut in half, 1 minced
>½ teaspoon crushed hot red pepper flakes (or to taste)
>¾ teaspoon salt
>1 bay leaf
>¼ cup red wine vinegar
>⅓ cup plum jam
>2 teaspoons minced cilantro
>Freshly ground black pepper

Soak the beans overnight in water to cover. The next day, drain and rinse them. Place in a large pot, cover with fresh water and bring to a boil with the halved garlic, ¼ teaspoon of the red pepper flakes, ¼ teaspoon of the salt, the bay leaf, and 2 tablespoons of the vinegar. Simmer until just tender, about 1 hour. Drain.

While the beans are still warm, stir in the minced garlic, ¼ teaspoon red pepper, ½ teaspoon salt, and 2 tablespoons vinegar, along with the plum jam, cilantro, and black pepper to taste. Serve at room temperature.

## HERBED KIDNEY BEANS
### (Lobio Mtsvanilit)

Yet another popular version of *lobio*.

SERVES 6 TO 8

> ½ pound dried kidney beans
> ¼ cup olive oil
> ¼ cup red wine vinegar
> 1 teaspoon ground coriander seed
> ½ cup mixed chopped fresh herbs (cilantro, parsley, basil, dill, tarragon)
> Salt
> Freshly ground black pepper

Soak the beans overnight in water to cover. The next day, drain and rinse them. Place in a large pot and cover with fresh water. Add ½ teaspoon salt. Bring the water to a boil and simmer until the beans are tender, about 1 hour. Drain. While the beans are still warm, stir in the remaining ingredients, adding salt and pepper to taste.

Allow the beans to cool to room temperature before serving.

# BEET PURÉE
## (Charkhlis Mkhali)

$A$ hallmark of Georgian cuisine is *mkhali* (or, colloquially, *pkhali*), a vegetable purée to which herbs and ground walnuts are added. *Mkhali* is made from any number of different vegetables, though spinach and beets are favored. Some of the most interesting versions call for radish and even cauliflower greens. Try experimenting with greens from the garden that might otherwise go to waste.

In making *mkhali,* you must rely on your palate, since the amount of vinegar necessary depends on the sugar content of each given vegetable. The purée should taste slightly sharp, but never vinegary.

Georgians insist that the real secret to a good *mkhali* is mixing it well by hand. Indeed, for the best flavor, experienced cooks prepare food whenever possible not just *by* hand, but *with* the hands. This careful mixing ensures that all ingredients are well incorporated and allows for perfect control of the texture. In deference to American style, my recipe calls for blending in the food processor. Should you have the time or inclination, however, by all means try mixing the *mkhali* by hand.

SERVES 6

1 pound beets
½ cup shelled walnuts
3 garlic cloves, peeled
½ teaspoon salt
½ cup chopped cilantro
½ cup chopped parsley
Freshly ground black pepper
¼ teaspoon dried summer savory
¼ teaspoon ground coriander seed
1 or 2 teaspoons red wine vinegar (to taste)

Bake the unpeeled beets at 375° F. for 1 to 1½ hours, until tender. (If you are short of time, the beets may be boiled, but their flavor will not be as good.) While the beets are cooking, grind together the walnuts, garlic, and salt. Add the cilantro and parsley and continue grinding to make a fine paste. Transfer to a bowl.

When the beets are soft, peel them and finely grate them in the food processor. In a medium bowl mix together the grated beets and the ground walnut mixture, then stir in the remaining ingredients. Keep tasting, as the amount of vinegar needed will depend on the sweetness of the beets. The *mkhali* should be slightly tart.

Chill in the refrigerator for at least 2 hours, but bring to room temperature before serving, mounded on a plate and cross-hatched on top with a knife.

VARIATIONS

For leek *mkhali,* clean well 1 pound of leeks and cut off all but 2 inches of the green tops. Boil gently in salted water for 20 to 25 minutes, then drain and purée in a food processor. Follow directions for beet *mkhali,* substituting 1 tablespoon minced fresh dill for the ground coriander seed.

For a *mkhali* of greens, use 1 pound of greens (spinach, beet, radish, or cauliflower). Wash the greens well and cook, covered, in the water left clinging to the leaves until tender, 5 to 20 minutes, depending on the variety. Squeeze out the excess moisture, then mince finely. Follow the directions for beet *mkhali,* seasoning to taste. (In general, the greens call for a bit less salt and coriander seed.)

# BEETS WITH CHERRY SAUCE
## (Charkhlis Chogi)

These wonderful beets are simultaneously sweet and tangy. In Georgia, cornelian cherries are used, but our tart domestic cherries provide similar savor. *Chogi* is usually eaten warm or at room temperature, but I like it best as a refreshing salad, lightly chilled.

SERVES 2 TO 3

    1 pound beets
    1 medium onion, peeled and minced
    1 tablespoon butter
    1/3 cup tart dried cherries
    10 tablespoons water
    2 tablespoons minced parsley
    2 tablespoons minced cilantro or dill
    1/8 teaspoon salt

Preheat the oven to 375° F.

Scrub the beets but do not peel. Bake until tender, 1 to 1½ hours.

Meanwhile, sauté the onion in the butter until soft, 10 to 15 minutes.

Simmer the cherries in the water until very soft, about 15 minutes. Force through a sieve or food mill, adding additional water, if necessary, to make ¼ cup of thick sauce.

When the beets are ready, peel and slice them thinly. Place in a bowl and add the cooked onion and cherry sauce. Stir in the minced herbs and salt.

N O T E : *Chogi* tastes best when served the same day it is made.

# CABBAGE WITH WALNUTS
## (Kombostos Ruleti Nigvzit)

One of the most tempting ways the Georgians serve vegetables is stuffed. The typical Georgian table displays stuffed carrots, quince, and pumpkin along with the more familiar cabbage leaves, peppers, and tomatoes. Not surprisingly, the favored filling is a zesty mixture of walnuts and spices. The vegetable container is always cooked as briefly as possible to retain its fresh flavor. Unlike the Eastern European method of preparation that calls for prolonged cooking of the stuffed leaves, the cabbage here serves mainly as a foil for the aromatic filling. This walnut filling may be used to stuff virtually any favorite vegetable—just be careful not to overcook it.

SERVES 6 TO 8

> 1 small head white cabbage
> 3 heaping cups shelled walnuts
> ¾ teaspoon whole coriander seed
> ¾ teaspoon ground marigold
> Scant 1½ teaspoons salt
> 4 small garlic cloves, peeled and roughly chopped
> 3 sprigs cilantro
> Pinch cayenne
> Pinch dried fenugreek
> 1 tablespoon red wine vinegar
> 6 tablespoons mixed chopped fresh herbs (parsley, cilantro, dill, celery leaf)
> Pomegranate seeds

Core the cabbage and cook in a large pot of boiling water until the leaves are tender, about 25 minutes. Drain well.

Meanwhile, prepare the filling: Grind the walnuts very fine. In a mortar with a pestle, pound into a paste the coriander seed, marigold, salt, garlic, cilantro, and a pinch each of cayenne and fenugreek. Stir into the walnuts, then add the vinegar. Stir in the mixed chopped herbs and mix well.

Carefully separate the head of cabbage into leaves. Working with one leaf at a time, cut out the tough rib, then mound about 1 tablespoon of the walnut filling in the center of the leaf and roll it up to make a packet. Repeat with the remaining leaves. Cut each cabbage roll in half on the diagonal to reveal the filling. Serve at room temperature, garnished with pomegranate seeds.

VARIATIONS

*Stuffed Carrots.* If you are lucky enough to find broad, blunt-ended carrots, they make excellent containers for stuffing. To fill carrots, trim and peel 2 pounds of them. Boil whole for 15 to 20 minutes, until tender but still firm. Carefully scoop out the insides, leaving a shell at least ¼ inch thick, and stuff the carrots with the filling. If the carrots are long and thin, as most American varieties are, slice them lengthwise after boiling. Scoop out the soft inner core to make boats. Spread the filling in the hollows.

*Stuffed Eggplant.* Try to find the small Japanese variety of eggplant. Boil 2 pounds of eggplant whole, until just tender. With a vegetable corer, scoop out the insides. Stuff the eggplants with the filling, then slice them and arrange on a platter. If using large globe eggplants, slice the eggplant and sauté in olive oil. Drain on paper toweling and spread with the filling.

# EGGPLANT WITH GARLIC
## (Badridzhani Nivrit)

Eggplant, garlic, and cilantro blend appealingly in this homey dish.

SERVES 4 TO 6

**1 large (1¼-pound) eggplant**
**Salt**
**¾ cup olive oil (approximately)**
**3 large garlic cloves, peeled and roughly chopped**
**Chopped cilantro**

Slice the unpeeled eggplant into rounds ½ inch thick, then cut each round in half crosswise. Sprinkle with salt and let drain on paper toweling for at least 30 minutes. Rinse and pat dry.

In a large skillet heat 1 tablespoon of oil. Place some eggplant slices in the hot oil and cook over medium-low heat, covered, until soft and lightly browned, about 2 or 3 minutes. Turn the eggplant, add another tablespoon of oil to the pan, and cook, covered, for another 2 or 3 minutes. Remove the eggplant slices from the oil and drain well. Repeat with the remaining eggplant, adding oil as necessary.

In a mortar with a pestle, pound 1 teaspoon salt and the garlic to make a paste. Spread this paste lightly on the cooked eggplant pieces; let sit for 1 minute, then gently scrape most of the paste off. Place the eggplant on a dish and serve at room temperature, garnished with chopped cilantro.

# HERBED EGGPLANT SALAD
## (Badridzhani Mtsvanilit)

This salad goes well with grilled poultry or meat. It is wise to salt the eggplant here to ensure that it is not bitter. Otherwise the aromatic taste of the spices and herbs will be lost.

SERVES 6

- 1 large (1¼-pound) eggplant
- 1 medium onion, peeled and minced
- 2 tablespoons olive oil
- Generous ½ cup shelled walnuts
- 2 large garlic cloves, peeled
- ½ teaspoon ground coriander seed
- ½ teaspoon ground marigold
- ½ teaspoon dried fenugreek
- Pinch cayenne
- ¾ teaspoon salt
- ¾ cup finely chopped mixed fresh herbs (cilantro, celery leaf, parsley, dill)
- 2 teaspoons red wine vinegar

Slice the eggplant lengthwise, sprinkle it with salt, and leave it to drain on paper toweling for at least 30 minutes. Rinse and pat dry.

Preheat the oven to 500° F.

Place the eggplant pieces cut side down on an oiled baking sheet. Bake for 20 minutes, or until tender.

Sauté the onion in the olive oil until golden. Set aside.

Finely grind the walnuts with the garlic and spices. Turn out into a bowl and stir in the cooked onions. Add the chopped herbs and the wine vinegar.

Let the eggplant cool to lukewarm, then remove the skin and cut the pulp into 1-inch pieces. Mix the eggplant thoroughly with the nut mixture. Cool to room temperature before serving.

# STUFFED EGGPLANT
## (Badridzhani Bostneulis Satenit)

A simple and elegant way to highlight a number of garden vegetables, this excellent dish is like *imam bayeldi* with a Georgian flair.

SERVES 8 TO 10

  4 eggplants (2 pounds total)
  1 large red pepper, cored and seeded
  1 small onion, peeled
  2 tablespoons each minced cilantro, parsley, and basil
  ¼ cup chopped celery leaves
  4 garlic cloves, peeled and minced
  Diced hot red or green pepper
  5 medium tomatoes
  1 teaspoon salt
  ¼ teaspoon freshly ground black pepper
  ¼ cup corn oil

Cut the eggplants in half lengthwise and with a spoon scrape out most of the seeds, creating a hollow in each half.

Dice the red pepper and the onion. Place them in a bowl with the minced herbs, celery leaves, garlic, and hot pepper to taste. Peel, seed, and chop the tomatoes; add to the other vegetables. Stir in the salt, pepper, and 2 tablespoons of the oil. Mix well.

Stuff the eggplants with this mixture and place in a large skillet. Add about ¼ cup water to the bottom of the pan. Drizzle the eggplant halves with the remaining 2 tablespoons of oil. Cover the skillet and simmer for 45 minutes, or until the eggplant is tender.

To serve, slice each stuffed half eggplant in half lengthwise.

# EGGPLANT CAVIAR
## (Badridzhnis Khizilala)

Strictly speaking, this eggplant preparation is native not to Georgia but to the Caucasus region in general. This is such a good recipe, however, that I am including it anyway, precision aside. The "caviar" may be eaten plain or spread on slices of black bread.

SERVES 12

- 3 small eggplants (about 2½ pounds total)
- 2 medium onions, peeled and finely chopped
- ½ cup olive oil
- 1 green pepper, cored, seeded, and finely chopped
- 4 garlic cloves, peeled and crushed
- 3 large tomatoes, peeled and finely chopped (or one 28-ounce can plum tomatoes, drained and finely chopped)
- 1 generous teaspoon honey
- 1 tablespoon salt
- Freshly ground black pepper
- Juice of 1 lemon

Place the eggplants in an ovenproof dish and bake in a preheated 375° F. oven until tender, about 45 minutes. Set aside to cool.

Meanwhile, sauté the onions in the olive oil until soft but not brown. Add the chopped green pepper and the garlic; cook until the green pepper begins to soften, 10 to 15 minutes.

Peel the baked eggplants and chop the pulp finely. Add to the frying pan along with the chopped tomatoes, honey, salt, and pepper. Bring the mixture to a boil, cover, and reduce the heat to low. Simmer for about 1 hour.

Remove the cover from the frying pan and continue to simmer the mixture until all the excess liquid has evaporated from the pan and the mixture is thick but not dry. Stir occasionally. This final simmering will take 20 to 45 minutes, depending on the consistency of the vegetables. When the mixture is ready, stir in the lemon juice and taste for seasoning, adding black pepper liberally.

Transfer the mixture to a bowl and chill, covered, in the refrigerator for several hours or overnight.

# POTATO PANCAKE
### (Labda)

*Labda* is a Passover specialty of the Georgian Jews, but this large, rich pancake makes a quick and filling supper any time of year.

**SERVES 8**

> 1 pound boiling potatoes
> 1 cup finely chopped walnuts
> 2 tablespoons finely chopped parsley
> ½ teaspoon salt
> Freshly ground pepper
> 3 large eggs, beaten
> 2 tablespoons butter
> 2 tablespoons corn oil

Boil the potatoes until tender; peel and mash them. Stir in the walnuts, parsley, salt, pepper to taste, and eggs, mixing well.

In a 10-inch skillet with sloping sides, melt 1 tablespoon each of butter and oil. When hot, spoon the pancake batter into the pan, pressing down with a spatula to form an even cake. Cook over medium high heat for about 4 minutes, or until the bottom of the pancake is brown and crusty. Slide the pancake onto a platter. Melt the remaining butter and oil in the skillet, then invert the pancake into the skillet and fry the other side until brown, about 4 minutes more. Slide out onto a platter and serve, cut into wedges.

# MUSHROOMS IN CREAM
## (Soko Arazhanit)

Cooked slowly in heavy cream with herbs and spices, these mushrooms acquire a deep, mellow taste.

SERVES 4

> 1 tablespoon butter
> 1 pound mushrooms, trimmed and thickly sliced
> Salt
> Freshly ground black pepper
> 1½ cups heavy cream
> 4 handfuls each (about 2 ounces each) parsley and dill sprigs
> 5 whole black peppercorns
> One 2-inch piece cinnamon stick
> 2 bay leaves
> 3 whole cloves

Melt the butter in a saucepan and toss the mushrooms in it just long enough to coat them. Season lightly with salt and pepper to taste.

Heat the cream to boiling and pour over the mushrooms.

Tie the remaining ingredients into cheesecloth and add to the mushrooms.

Cover and simmer the mixture for 45 to 50 minutes, or until the liquid is absorbed. Remove the cheesecloth bag and serve.

# WILD MUSHROOMS, TELAVI STYLE
## (Khis Soko)

In the spring, a special variety of large, edible mushrooms appears on the trees around Telavi, Kakheti's main city, providing occasion to eat a well-loved dish not unlike the *chirbuli* of western Georgia. Because the same mushrooms do not grow in the United States, my recipe calls for shiitake mushrooms or morels, but I caution that this dish will taste only as interesting as the mushrooms you choose. They should be strongly flavored, with firm texture; made with regular field champignons, *khis soko* is unexceptional.

SERVES 4

> 1 pound flavorful mushrooms, such as shiitake or morels
> 3 eggs, lightly beaten
> 2 tablespoons minced cilantro
> 1 tablespoon minced mint
> 2 tablespoons minced scallion
> ¼ teaspoon salt
> Freshly ground black pepper
> 3 tablespoons butter

Finely chop the mushrooms. Beat the eggs and combine them with the cilantro, mint, scallion, salt, and pepper.

In a large skillet melt the butter and cook the mushrooms quickly over high heat. Do not allow them to give off liquid. Add the egg mixture and stir until the eggs are just cooked through. Serve immediately.

# POTATOES WITH WALNUTS
## *(Kartopili Nigvzit)*

Here is an exotic variation on the usual potato salad dressed with mayonnaise or vinaigrette.

SERVES 4 TO 6

> 1 pound boiling potatoes
> 1 medium onion, peeled and minced
> 1 tablespoon butter
> 1 cup shelled walnuts
> 2 garlic cloves, peeled
> 1 teaspoon salt
> Freshly ground black pepper
> ¼ cup finely chopped mixed herbs (cilantro, parsley, dill)
> 2 tablespoons red wine vinegar
> Parsley

Boil the potatoes in salted water until tender.

Meanwhile, sauté the onion lightly in the butter.

Finely grind the walnuts with the garlic, salt, and pepper to taste. Stir in the herbs and vinegar. Add the cooked onion.

While the potatoes are still warm, peel them and cut into eighths. Stir together thoroughly with the nut mixture (the potatoes will begin to break up). Serve at room temperature, garnished with parsley.

# STEAMED PURSLANE
## (Danduri)

Purslane is prized in Georgia even as it is unknown as an edible in America. American gardeners consider this plant invasive, but perhaps we could learn from the Georgians. Purslane contains more Omega-3, a cholesterol-reducing oil, than any other leafy green vegetable. And it has a fresh, lemony taste that complements such bitter salad greens as chicory and arugula. Georgians serve purslane fresh in salads or lightly cooked and seasoned, as in this recipe.

Rinse stalks of fresh purslane well and place in a saucepan with 1 inch of water. Bring to a boil and simmer the purslane, covered, for 3 to 5 minutes, until tender but not limp. Drain well.

Season the purslane with salt, freshly ground pepper, and minced garlic to taste. Drizzle with olive oil and red wine vinegar. Serve hot or at room temperature.

# STUFFED TOMATOES
## (Pamidvris Tolma)

These tomatoes packed with fresh herbs and walnuts differ from most other stuffed vegetables in that they contain no meat or starch. They work equally well as an accompaniment to grilled meat or as a featured luncheon entrée. Serve crusty bread on the side.

SERVES 4

- 1 onion, peeled and minced
- 2 tablespoons butter
- 1 cup shelled walnuts
- 4 garlic cloves, peeled
- ¾ teaspoon ground coriander seed
- ¾ teaspoon ground marigold
- ¾ teaspoon salt
- Freshly ground black pepper
- ¼ teaspoon paprika
- ⅛ teaspoon cayenne
- 1 cup boiling water
- 2 tablespoons red wine vinegar
- 4 large firm tomatoes
- ¾ cup finely chopped mixed fresh herbs (basil, cilantro, parsley)
- Cilantro

In a deep saucepan just large enough to hold the tomatoes, cook the onion in the butter until soft. Finely grind ½ cup of walnuts with 3 garlic cloves. Add to the cooked onions. Stir in the ground coriander seed, marigold, ½ teaspoon salt, ¼ teaspoon pepper, the paprika, and cayenne. Pour in the boiling water and the vinegar and simmer for 10 minutes.

Meanwhile, slice the tops off the tomatoes and scrape out the seeds, being careful not to puncture the skin.

Grind together the remaining ½ cup walnuts, garlic clove, salt, and pepper. Stir in the finely chopped herbs. Stuff the tomatoes with this mixture and replace the tops.

Place the tomatoes in the nut sauce and cook them over low heat, covered, until they are tender but still hold their shape, about 25 minutes. Allow to cool to room temperature in the pan.

Serve the tomatoes on a bed of the sauce, garnished with sprigs of cilantro.

## STEWED GREEN TOMATOES
### (Mtsvane Pamidori)

This is a tasty and colorful way to consume late summer's unripened crop of tomatoes.

SERVES 4

> 2 tablespoons olive oil
> 1 pound green tomatoes, coarsely chopped
> 1 medium onion, peeled and finely chopped
> 2 large carrots, peeled and cut into rounds
> ¼ cup coarsely chopped parsley
> ¼ cup coarsely chopped celery leaves
> ¼ cup water
> 3 garlic cloves, peeled and roughly chopped
> 1 teaspoon salt
> Freshly ground black pepper

In a skillet, heat the olive oil. Add the chopped tomatoes, onion, carrots, parsley, celery leaves, and the water. Cover the skillet and cook over low heat, stirring occasionally, for 30 minutes.

In a mortar with a pestle, pound the garlic with the salt until a paste is formed.

When the vegetables are tender, remove from the heat and stir in the garlic paste and pepper to taste.

Cool to room temperature before serving.

# VEGETABLE MEDLEY
### (Adzhapsandali)

*Adzhapsandali* is my favorite eggplant dish. It is similar to a rata-touille, but it bites back. If you prefer something less fiery, simply reduce the amount of cayenne.

SERVES 4 TO 6

   1 pound eggplant
   1 large boiling potato
   1 medium onion, peeled and chopped
   2 tablespoons corn oil
   1½ pounds tomatoes
   1 medium green pepper, cored, seeded, and chopped
   4 garlic cloves, peeled and minced
   Generous 2 tablespoons minced dill
   Generous 2 tablespoons minced cilantro
   Generous 2 tablespoons minced parsley
   Generous 2 tablespoons minced basil
   ¾ teaspoon salt
   ¼ teaspoon paprika
   ¼ teaspoon cayenne (or less, to taste)
   ¼ teaspoon freshly ground black pepper

Pierce the eggplant and bake it in a preheated 375° F. oven for 35 to 40 minutes, until tender. Allow to cool.

Meanwhile, boil the potato in salted water until just tender. Cool, then peel and cube.

Sauté the onion in the oil until soft.

Drop the tomatoes into boiling water and cook them until soft, about 10 minutes. Drain, then force through a sieve to make a purée. Add the tomato purée to the onion along with the green pepper and the minced garlic. Simmer uncovered for 10 minutes, until slightly thickened.

Peel the eggplant and cut it into cubes. Add the cubes to the tomato mixture along with the cubed potato. Stir in the remaining ingredients and heat gently for 5 minutes more. Cool to room temperature before serving.

See also: Cauliflower with Egg (page 129), Green Beans with Egg (page 130), Herbed Potatoes with Eggs (page 132), Eggplant with Cheese and Yogurt (page 133), Spinach with Yogurt (page 134), and Wild Mushrooms, Telavi Style (page 171).

**Woman with a Tankard of Beer**

# PICKLES
# AND
# PRESERVES

**P**ickles and preserves feature prominently on the Georgian table. Pungent vegetables complement the rich taste of cheese and nut dishes, while sugary preserves serve as the perfect send-off to an extravagant meal. In the spring, Georgians forage for the tender shoots of wild vegetables, which they pack in brine to enjoy later in the year. Larger, cultivated vegetables are often stuffed with walnuts and herbs before pickling. As for sweet preparations, Georgians like their fruits preserved whole in syrup—jelly, even jam, does not seem toothsome enough. Cooked briefly in heavy syrup, the fruits glisten gemlike when served in glass dishes. These preserves are not sidelights to a meal, but highly anticipated treats for breakfast, tea, or dessert.

## PICKLED CABBAGE ROSE
### (Mzhave Kombosto)

**C**abbage is one of the easiest vegetables to pickle at home. A whole head is often soured in vinegar with beets, which tint the pale leaves a deep pink. By turning back each leaf individually before immersing the cabbage in brine, you can form a spectacular "rose" to grace the table on special occasions.

SERVES 8 TO 10

> 1 small head white cabbage, about 1½ pounds
> 3 medium raw beets, peeled and diced
> 3 ribs celery, including leaves, diced
> 8 sprigs parsley
> One 4-inch piece dried hot red pepper

10 black peppercorns
1 teaspoon paprika
6½ cups red wine vinegar
7½ cups boiling water

Four days before serving, remove the outer leaves from the cabbage and make an X at the base of the core. Place the cabbage in a large pot of cold water and bring to a boil. Simmer until just tender, 35 to 40 minutes. Drain in a colander and rinse under cold water until cool enough to handle.

Place the cabbage on a flat surface. Working carefully with one leaf at a time, bend back each leaf as far as it will go without breaking off from the core. Continue with each subsequent leaf until the entire head of cabbage has been opened up to form a "rose."

In a large saucepan, combine the beets, celery, parsley, hot pepper, peppercorns, paprika, and vinegar. Bring to a boil and simmer for 5 minutes.

Place the cabbage in a large stainless steel or enamel pot (a 6-quart dutch oven is the right size). Pour the vinegar mixture over the cabbage, then add the boiling water, just to cover. Place a plate on top of the cabbage, weighting it so that the cabbage is completely immersed. Leave unrefrigerated in a cool spot for 4 days.

To serve, chill the cabbage in the refrigerator in its pickling liquid (it will keep for 4 days), then lift it out onto a platter. Cut into wedges to serve.

# RED PEPPER PICKLE
## (Mzhave Bulgaruli Tsitsaka)

This is an aromatic pickle with a pleasing sweet-and-sour taste. It can accompany meat or simply be piled on a slice of crusty bread, which is how I like to eat it.

MAKES 4 PINTS

> 2 pounds red bell peppers
> 2½ cups red wine vinegar
> 2½ cups corn oil
> 2 whole large heads garlic, peeled and minced
> 2 cups minced cilantro
> 1 cup minced parsley

Quarter the peppers and seed them. Place on a baking sheet skin side up and put under the broiler until the skins have blackened. Remove to paper bags to cool, then peel off the skins. Slice the peppers into strips.

In a saucepan, bring the vinegar and corn oil to a simmer. Add the garlic and herbs. Simmer 5 minutes, stir in the pepper strips, and simmer 15 minutes longer, stirring occasionally. Remove the pan from the heat and cover. Let stand overnight. The following day, pour into sterilized jars. The pickle tastes best when left to sit, refrigerated, for 3 days before using. Store in the refrigerator. Keeps 1 month.

# HOT PEPPER RELISH
## (Adzhika)

No Georgian cook would think of serving grilled or roasted meat plain, without any sort of condiment or garnish. While the number of sauces to choose from is legion, another way to enliven meat is with the hot pepper relish, *adzhika*. *Adzhika* varies in consistency from a rather stiff, dry paste to a liquidy concoction like salsa. In the western province of Samegrelo, *adzhika* is served with melon, the coolness of the fruit cutting its fire. This recipe yields a fresh, salsalike relish.

MAKES ABOUT 1 PINT

    8 garlic cloves, peeled
    1 large celery stalk, including leaves
    ¼ pound fresh hot red peppers, including seeds
    1 large red bell pepper, cored and seeded
    2 cups coarsely chopped fresh dill
    1½ cups coarsely chopped cilantro
    ⅓ cup red wine vinegar
    ¼ teaspoon salt

Using the pulse control of a food processor, grind the garlic slightly. Coarsely chop the celery, hot peppers, and red bell pepper and add them to the garlic. Pulse again. Add the chopped herbs and pulse to a medium coarseness. Transfer the mixture to a bowl and stir in the vinegar and salt. Cover and let stand overnight before packing into jars. Either store in the refrigerator or process in a water bath for longer storage. This relish tastes best when allowed to sit for 3 days before serving.

# PICKLED LEEKS
## (Mzhave Prasi)

Georgians enjoy the tang of many vegetables, such as leeks, that are unfamiliar to Americans in pickled form. Aged in vinegar, leeks make a crisp and unusual pickle. For best results, use tiny leeks culled from the garden, preferably no larger than 1½ inches in diameter.

MAKES 1 QUART

- 1 pound small leeks
- 1 stalk celery, coarsely chopped
- 1 large carrot, peeled and cut into rounds
- 2 small hot red or green peppers, seeded and halved
- 3 garlic cloves, peeled
- 1 bay leaf
- 2 tablespoons salt
- 2 cups white wine vinegar

Rinse the leeks well to remove any grit, trim the root ends and tops, and place in a large bowl. Pour boiling water over the leeks and let stand for 1 minute. Drain and rinse well with cold water.

Pack the leeks upright into a tall, sterile quart jar along with the celery, carrot, hot peppers, garlic, bay leaf, and salt.

Pour the vinegar over the vegetables, making sure they are covered (add more vinegar if necessary). Seal the jar. Allow the pickle to stand at cool room temperature for at least 3 weeks before serving. Store in the refrigerator after opening.

# PICKLED GARLIC
## *(Mzhave Niori)*

This pickle is a garlic-lover's delight. Georgians nibble large quantities of these cloves as appetizers, but less adventurous eaters may use them to invigorate salads or stews.

MAKES 1 PINT

> 2 large heads garlic, unpeeled
> 1 tablespoon salt
> ½ cup unsweetened pomegranate juice
> ⅔ cup white wine vinegar
> Black peppercorns (optional)
> Red pepper flakes (optional)

Place the garlic heads in a sterile pint jar and sprinkle with the salt. In a small saucepan, bring the pomegranate juice and vinegar to a boil. Pour over the garlic. If desired, add a few peppercorns or red pepper flakes. Make sure the garlic is completely covered by the liquid (use a crumpled piece of aluminum foil to keep it submerged, if necessary). Seal the jar. Store at cool room temperature for at least 3 weeks before eating (the flavor improves upon standing).

To serve, with a sharp knife cut all the way around the outer skin of the garlic about ½ inch up from the base of the bulb. The outer skin should slide off easily from the top, revealing the tightly-packed cloves in a perfect head.

# GEORGIAN SPICE MIX
## (*Khmeli-Suneli*)

*Khmeli-suneli* is to Georgian cuisine what curry powder is to Indian. No set formula exists for making this mixture, as the proportions of herbs change to complement whatever dish is being prepared. Sometimes it is convenient to have a ready-made mixture on hand, though. This rendition of *khmeli-suneli* is quite basic. Try rubbing some on steak before grilling, or adding a teaspoon or two to beans or stew.

MAKES ABOUT ¼ CUP

   2 teaspoons ground coriander seed
   2 teaspoons dried basil
   2 teaspoons dried dillweed
   2 teaspoons dried summer savory
   1 teaspoon dried parsley
   1 teaspoon dried mint
   1 teaspoon dried fenugreek leaves
   1 teaspoon ground marigold
   1 bay leaf, crushed

In a mortar with a pestle, pound the spices together to a fine powder. Store airtight.

# FEIJOA RELISH
## *(Pheidzhoas Muraba)*

The wonderful feijoa is a tropical fruit belonging to the same family as eucalyptus. Its flavor suggests a hint of menthol along with ripe, aromatic grapes. Feijoa may be cooked into a jam, but its intense flavor is best preserved by mixing it raw with sugar into a vitamin-rich concoction. This relish is like a coarse, fresh jam.

MAKES 1 PINT

2 pounds ripe feijoas (see page 49)
2 pounds sugar

Pare the feijoas and put through a meat grinder with the sugar. Pack into sterile jars and seal.

# LADY APPLE PRESERVES
## (Samotkhis Vashlis Muraba)

Georgia's fruits are so lush that a popular saying goes, "If fruits had mouths they would eat themselves." Here, delicate lady apples are cooked into a lovely, mallow pink preserve. Be sure to use unwaxed apples so that the syrup can penetrate the skin.

MAKES 1 QUART

1 pound lady apples
2¼ cups sugar
2 cups water

Leaving stems intact, pierce the apples all over with a thin skewer and place in a pot. Cover with boiling water and put a plate on top to keep the apples submerged. Let stand for 15 minutes.

Meanwhile, make the syrup. In a heavy saucepan combine the sugar and 2 cups water. Bring to a boil, stirring until the sugar dissolves.

Transfer the apples to the boiling syrup and stir for a minute to coat them. Lower the heat and cook, covered, for 15 minutes. Remove the lid and increase the heat to medium high. Cook rapidly, turning the apples occasionally, for 10 to 15 minutes more, until the fruit is tender but has not lost its shape. Pack with the syrup into a sterilized jar and seal.

# CORNELIAN
# CHERRY PRESERVES
### (Shindis Muraba)

This pleasingly tart preserve may be made with sour (morello) cherries if cornelian cherries are unavailable. It is unnecessary to remove the small pits in cornelian cherries before cooking, but if sour cherries are used, they should be pitted. Variations on this preserve are found throughout the Middle East (interestingly, the Georgian word *muraba* has counterparts in both Persian and Hindi).

MAKES 2 PINTS

4 cups sugar
2½ cups water
1 pound cornelian cherries

In a large kettle, bring the sugar and water to a boil, stirring until the sugar dissolves. Simmer for 15 minutes. Stir in the cherries and simmer for about 30 minutes more, or until the syrup has thickened, periodically skimming the foam from the surface. Pour into sterile jars and seal.

# FRUIT LEATHER
## (*Tklapi*)

**W**herever a rare natural widening occurs along the mountain high-ways, local residents sit by the roadside hawking their foods and crafts —plums and apples, peaches and apricots, colorful knitted mittens and socks. These roadside stands sell the best *tklapi*, fruit leather made from the *tkemali* plum that is the favored souring agent for soups and stews.

For snacking, Georgians enjoy a sweet fruit leather of apricots or peaches, made following the same procedure as for sour *tklapi*. An excellent though untraditional fruit leather may also be prepared from the juice used in making the walnut roll, *churchkhela*.

To make sour *tklapi:* Take ripe sour plums, cut them in half, and remove the pits. Place in a saucepan, add just enough water so that they won't burn, and bring to a boil. Reduce heat and cook slowly, covered, until the fruit is soft. Place the cooked plums in a sieve to drain, then purée in a food mill.

Place several smooth layers of newspaper on a table and top them with a piece of baking parchment. If the parchment has been folded and is creased, iron it gently.

Working quickly, spread the plum purée about ¹⁄₁₆ inch thick onto the parchment sheet, leaving 2 inches free at one end. Leave to dry for 24 hours.

The following day, attach clothespins to the free end of the parchment sheet and hang it on a clothesline in a breezy spot. Leave to dry for 1 to 2 days more, bringing the *tklapi* in at night. (If you do not have access to the outdoors, or if the weather is bad, the *tklapi* may be dried in a 200° F. oven for 6 to 10 hours, until it is no longer tacky to the touch.)

When the fruit leather is dry, place it on a flat surface, parchment side up. Soak the parchment with a wet sponge, then slowly peel it away from the leather.

Store tightly wrapped. Cut off pieces of fruit leather as needed.

To make a sweet *tklapi:* To each 1 cup of juice mixture left over from making *churchkhela* (page 192), add ¼ cup unsweetened apricot juice (available in health-food stores). Heat the juices to simmering. Pour onto baking parchment as described above (2 cups of leftover *chur-chkhela* juice will cover an 8- x 10-inch piece of parchment). Follow the remaining directions for drying the *tklapi*.

To store sweet *tklapi*, dust with cornstarch and roll. Keep tightly sealed in plastic wrap.

Five Princes Carousing

# S W E E T S

eorgians do not regularly eat desserts, since their wonderful fruits, either fresh or cooked into preserves, satisfy most cravings for sugar. But on special occasions, pastries and cakes are enjoyed. Some of these are European imports, introduced through Russia; others are typical of oriental confections, dripping with honey. A third category of sweets includes vegetables or grains, ritual foods that were traditionally served at wakes or other religious repasts. The most distinctive desserts, however, use walnuts and grapes, the indigenous products that give such notable character to Georgian cuisine.

## C A N D I E D   W A L N U T S
### (*Gozinaki*)

At the New Year, honey augurs the sweetness of the year to come. Sometimes a honeycomb is symbolically touched to children's lips, but all the Georgian children I know would rather eat *gozinaki*, the New Year's treat of nuts candied in honey. *Gozinaki* keeps well, a convenience considering that the New Year's feasting often runs on and on. On January 14, Georgians celebrate a second New Year, based on the old-style Julian calendar still observed by the Orthodox Church.

MAKES ABOUT 2 DOZEN PIECES OF CANDY

  3½ cups shelled walnuts
  1 cup honey

Toast the walnuts lightly at 350° F. for 10 minutes, then chop them coarsely.

In a deep saucepan bring the honey to a boil. Stir in the nuts and cook over medium heat for 8 to 10 minutes, stirring periodically, until the mixture is thick. Be careful not to let it burn.

Pour the mixture out onto a moistened wooden board or oiled marble slab. With a spatula, spread it ½ inch thick. When cool, cut into 2-inch diamonds.

N O T E : This recipe was tested by the kitchen staff at *Eating Well* magazine, who experimented with alternative cooking methods to come up with a Western variation. For crisper *gozinaki,* shape the cooked mass into a rectangle on a parchment-lined baking sheet and bake at 350° F. for 10 minutes. When cool, cut the candy into diamonds as directed.

# WALNUT ROLL
## (Churchkhela)

*Churchkhela* is a long string of nuts that have been dipped repeatedly in concentrated fresh grape juice *(badagi)* to form a confection. Sami Zubaida, an authority on Iraqi cuisine, remembers a similar preparation from his childhood, which he and his friends called a "judge's prick." I encountered no similar moniker in Georgia; however, Georgian soldiers did carry *churchkhela* on their military campaigns, since a single piece contains enough calories for a whole day. What's more, the longer it's kept, the more concentrated and full of energy-rich sugars it becomes. *Churchkhela* is made either with whole nuts or halves, walnuts or hazelnuts. Although time-consuming, it is well worth the effort.

**MAKES 2 STRANDS**

> **40 walnut halves (or whole hazelnuts)**
> **1½ quarts white grape juice**
> **¾ cup sugar**
> **1 cup flour**
> **Confectioners' sugar**

Thread a needle with a 30-inch length of heavy-duty thread. Knot the ends together. With the flat side of the nuts facing up, thread 20 walnut halves onto the thread, then thread the remaining walnut halves flat side down. (It's easier to thread them through the thinnest portion of the nut, rather than through the ridge.)

Cut the thread from the needle and knot the ends. Then push half of the walnuts to that end of the thread, leaving about 6 inches of thread in between the 2 portions of nuts. Pick up the thread from the top. You will have 2 separate strands of walnut halves hanging flat side up.

In a large skillet combine the grape juice and sugar. Heat to just below the boiling point. Place the flour in a bowl and very gradually stir in the heated juice, whisking constantly so that no lumps form. When about half of the juice has been added to the flour, pour the remaining flour mixture into the skillet and bring to a boil, stirring. Simmer for 15 minutes, stirring occasionally, until the mixture has thickened slightly.

Meanwhile, find a board about 4 inches wide and suspend it between two chairs. Place newspaper on the floor underneath to catch the drips.

Pick up the walnuts by the middle of the thread and slowly dip them into the juice mixture, using a spoon to coat the top sides, if necessary. Slowly pull them up from the juice and carefully drape the thread over the prepared board so that the walnut strands hang down over the newspaper.

Allow the nuts to dry for 15 to 20 minutes, or until the coating is just slightly tacky. Then return the nuts to the juice, which has been kept warm, and repeat the dipping process. Allow to dry again for 20 minutes or so. (It helps to hang the nut strands in front of an open window, or to dry them in front of a fan if the weather is damp, although making *churchkhela* in humid weather is not recommended.) The drier the coating, the better the next layer will adhere.

Repeat the dipping process 8 to 10 times, or until the nuts are completely coated. Leave to dry for 3 to 4 days, until the strands are no longer sticky to the touch. When dry, pull out the strings and dust the *churchkhela* with confectioners' sugar.

To serve, cut the *churchkhela* into rounds.

N O T E : The leftover dipping juice may be made into a nontraditional *tklapi* or fruit leather (page 188).

# WALNUT-RAISIN TORTE
## (Nigvzis Torti)

This rich and impressive torte is like baklava with a cookie-dough crust. To intensify the raisiny flavor of the filling, the syrup is made from grape juice instead of honey.

SERVES 10 TO 12

½ pound (2 sticks) butter, softened
1 cup sugar
1 cup plain yogurt
3½ cups unbleached white flour
½ cup white grape juice

*FILLING*

2½ cups shelled walnuts
2 cups raisins
½ cup sugar
1 teaspoon ground cinnamon

In a bowl cream together the butter and ½ cup sugar; beat in the yogurt. Stir in the flour and mix well. Shape the dough into a ball and chill for at least 6 hours, or overnight.

Preheat the oven to 350° F. Toast the walnuts for 10 minutes until lightly browned, then grind them.

Steam the raisins over boiling water until plump. Mix with the ground walnuts and stir in ½ cup sugar and the cinnamon.

Divide the dough into 4 parts, keeping the unused dough refrigerated. On a floured board, roll out 1 piece of dough to a round 10 inches in diameter. Place it on a greased baking sheet. Cover to within 1 inch of the edges with ⅓ of the filling.

Roll out the second round and place it over the filling, then top with half of the remaining nut mixture. Roll out the third round and place it over the filling, then top with the remaining nut mixture. Cover with the last round of dough. Trim the edges and fold the top edge under to seal. Pat the pie into a uniform round shape and crimp the bottom edges with your fingers. Make 5 slits in the top crust.

Place in the oven and bake for 50 minutes, or until nicely browned.

Meanwhile, prepare a syrup by mixing together in a saucepan the remaining ½ cup sugar and the grape juice. Bring to a boil and simmer for 3 to 5 minutes, until a syrup forms.

When the pie is done, remove from the oven and allow to cool for 15 minutes. Then brush with the syrup to glaze, allowing it to soak into the filling through the slits in the crust. Set under a hot broiler for a minute to set the glaze.

Store any leftover cake tightly covered at room temperature.

# WALNUT PASTRY
## (*Pakhlava*)

One of the best desserts I tasted in Georgia is an East-West hybrid, the treasured recipe of Ira Kandelaki, whose mother was Russian and father Georgian. This cake is called *pakhlava*, but unlike its close cousin baklava, it is made with a modern Russian baking soda and sour cream dough rather than with phyllo. The result is a tender pastry with a devastatingly rich walnut filling. Serve in small portions.

SERVES 8 TO 10

12 tablespoons (1½ sticks) very cold unsalted butter
1¾ cups unbleached white flour
½ teaspoon baking soda
1 egg yolk
1 cup sour cream

*FILLING*

Heaping ½ cup shelled walnuts
1 cup sugar
½ teaspoon vanilla extract
2 egg whites

1 egg yolk, beaten

With a pastry blender or in a food processor, cut the butter into the flour and baking soda until it resembles coarse meal. Mix in the egg yolk and sour cream to make a soft dough. Wrap in wax paper and chill in the refrigerator for at least 2 hours.

Preheat the oven to 350° F. Grease and lightly flour a 9-inch square pan.

To make the filling, finely grind the walnuts; stir in the sugar and vanilla. Beat the egg whites until stiff but not dry and fold into the nut mixture.

Divide the chilled dough into 3 parts. Roll out the first piece of dough into a 9-inch square and transfer it to the pan. Spread with half of the filling, leaving a 1-inch border. Roll out the second piece of dough and carefully place it on top of the filling. Cover with the remaining filling. Roll out the last piece of dough, place it on top, and tuck the edges under slightly to seal. Flatten the pastry to conform to the sides of the pan. With a sharp knife, score the top of the pie lightly into diamonds.

Brush the top of the *pakhlava* with beaten egg yolk and bake for 45 to 50 minutes, until browned. Cut into diamonds to serve.

# BUTTER PASTRY
## (Kada)

One of the few traditional Georgian pastries is *kada,* a flaky, strudel-like dough filled with butter and sugar. The filling derives its rich flavor from flour cooked to a deep pink shade before the butter and sugar are stirred in. *Kada* is often rolled into a tight coil, but I like to leave the pastry in a ring so that it remains crisp and flaky. Don't be concerned if the filling oozes a bit during cooking. Simply mound fresh berries in the center of the ring before serving.

SERVES 8 TO 10

> 1½ cups unbleached white flour
> ¼ teaspoon salt
> Approximately ½ cup water
> 6 tablespoons (¾ stick) unsalted butter, melted

FILLING
> 2 tablespoons white flour
> 3 tablespoons unsalted butter
> ½ cup sugar
>
> 1 egg yolk, beaten

Place the flour in a large bowl and make a well in the middle. Add the salt and enough water to make a firm dough. Knead for 1 minute, then roll the dough out on a floured board to a 9- x 12-inch rectangle. Brush the dough with 2 tablespoons of the melted butter, fold it in quarters, wrap in wax paper, and chill for 10 to 15 minutes. Roll out the dough once again, brush it with 2 more tablespoons butter, fold, and chill. Repeat 1 more time and chill.

Meanwhile, prepare the filling. Place the flour in a skillet and fry over medium high heat, stirring constantly, until the flour turns a deep pink, bordering on brown. Do not allow the flour to burn. Add the butter and stir until the butter melts and the mixture is smooth. Remove from the heat, stir in the sugar, and cool.

Preheat the oven to 350° F. Dust a 10-inch pie plate with flour.

Roll the dough out into a 9- x 16-inch rectangle. Cover with filling to within 2 inches of the edges and roll up as for a jelly roll, starting from the long side. Using your hands, carefully stretch the roll to 28 inches.

Seal the seam of the roll with cold water, then carefully coil it into the pie plate, seam side down, forming a ring around the base of the plate. Bring the ends together and seal well. Brush the ring with the beaten egg yolk. Bake until lightly browned, 45 to 50 minutes. Remove from the pie plate while still warm and cool on a rack.

## "PEACHES"
### (Atami)

Here is a modern dessert, a playful tribute to Georgia's beloved peaches when they are not in season.

MAKES 6 CAKES, 1 PER PERSON

4 tablespoons (½ stick) unsalted butter, softened
¾ cup sugar
¼ teaspoon vanilla extract
⅛ teaspoon almond extract
1½ cups unbleached white flour
1½ teaspoons baking powder
Pinch salt
1 cup milk
2 egg whites

*SYRUP*
6 tablespoons white grape juice
3 tablespoons sugar

Peach jam
Red sugar sprinkles

Preheat the oven to 350° F. Liberally grease twelve 6-ounce custard cups. Place the cups on a cookie sheet.

Cream the butter with the sugar until fluffy; stir in the extracts. In another bowl combine the flour, baking powder, and salt. Add the flour mixture to the butter mixture alternately with the milk, beating well after each addition. Beat the egg whites until stiff but not dry. Fold into the batter.

Pour about ¼ cup of batter into each custard cup. Bake for 20 to 22 minutes, or just until a cake tester comes out clean. Do not let the cakes brown. Remove from the oven and immediately turn the cakes out onto a wire rack. Working quickly, turn each cake upright and with a serrated knife trim the crown of each cake to make a flat surface. (Discard the trimmings or save for a snack.)

Spread a thin layer of peach jam on the sliced end of each cake, and then press 2 cakes together to form a "peach." The cakes will stick together if they are still warm. If desired, gently press one end of each "peach" into a slightly pointed shape.

To make the syrup, combine the grape juice and sugar in a small saucepan. Bring to a boil and simmer for 5 minutes. With a pastry brush, brush each "peach" all over with syrup. Put the red sugar sprinkles in a bowl and dip the "peaches" into the sprinkles.

These cakes are best made early in the day or even a day before serving so that the syrup will soak in.

# LEMON TEA CAKE
## (Limnis Namtskhvari)

Another modern dessert that often graces urban tables is lemon tea cake, a light, dry cake that is not too filling. Using both yogurt and baking soda, it combines traditional Georgian and European baking methods.

SERVES 8

> 8 tablespoons (1 stick) unsalted butter, softened
> 1 cup confectioners' sugar
> 2 large eggs
> ½ cup plain yogurt
> 2 cups unbleached white flour
> ½ teaspoon baking soda
> ½ teaspoon salt
> Grated rind of 1 large lemon
> 4 teaspoons freshly squeezed lemon juice
> 1 tablespoon sugar

Preheat the oven to 350° F.

Cream together the butter and confectioners' sugar.

In a separate bowl, beat the eggs lightly; stir in the yogurt. Add this mixture to the creamed butter and sugar and beat with a whisk or in a mixer until light.

Sift the flour, baking soda, and salt into the batter. Stir in the grated lemon rind and juice. Turn the batter into an ungreased 7- x 11-inch pan.

Smooth the top of the batter and bake for 35 minutes, until golden. Allow the cake to cool in the pan. Cut into squares to serve. Fresh strawberries or raspberries lightly sweetened with sugar embellish this cake nicely.

# TEA CAKE
## (Chais Namtskhvari)

This delectable cake with a slight caramel flavor is quite literally a tea cake, since brewed black tea moistens the batter. The recipe is adapted from Tamara Sulakvelidze's Russian-Georgian cookbook.

SERVES 8 TO 10

> 2 heaping teaspoons loose black tea
> 1¼ cups boiling water
> 1½ cups sugar
> 2 eggs, separated
> 2 tablespoons unsalted butter, melted and cooled
> ½ cup plus 2 tablespoons plum jam
> 1 teaspoon baking soda
> ¼ cup red wine vinegar
> ¼ teaspoon salt
> 2 cups unbleached white flour
> ½ cup finely chopped toasted walnuts

Preheat the oven to 350° F. Grease a 9-inch round cake pan and dust it with flour.

Steep the tea in the boiling water for 15 minutes, then strain. You should have 1 cup of strong tea.

In a large skillet stir ½ cup sugar over medium high heat until it turns a light caramel color but is still in granules. Do not burn. Gradually add the tea, stirring constantly. When the sugar melts, remove the pan from the heat.

In a large bowl, beat the egg yolks with the remaining 1 cup sugar. Stir in the melted butter and 2 tablespoons jam. Beat in the tea mixture.

Dissolve the baking soda in the vinegar, then stir into the batter. Add the salt and flour and beat well.

Beat the egg whites until soft peaks form; fold them into the batter. Turn the batter into the prepared cake pan and bake until a tester comes out clean, 40 to 45 minutes. Cool the cake in the pan for 10 minutes, then invert onto a rack.

When cool, spread the top with the ½ cup jam and sprinkle the toasted nuts over it.

# H O N E Y   C A K E
## (Taplis Namtskhvari)

In a holdover from pagan times, as late as the last century rural Georgians believed illness to be a sign that the gods had taken up residence
in a mortal. The best way to cure the invalid was to appease the gods
with food. Superstitious families strewed the sick person's room with
fragrant petals and set a table with all sorts of appealing confections,
hoping thereby to satiate the gods and send them packing. Favored
delicacies included sweets made with honey, such as this honey cake.
Slightly dry and chewy, it need not be relegated to the sick room.

SERVES 10 TO 12

> 3 cups unbleached white flour
> 1 cup sugar
> 1 teaspoon ground cinnamon
> ¼ teaspoon ground cloves
> ¼ teaspoon ground coriander seed
> 1 teaspoon baking soda
> ¼ teaspoon salt
> 4 eggs, beaten
> 1 cup honey
> ⅓ cup chopped nuts (walnuts or almonds)

Preheat the oven to 325° F. Grease a 10-inch springform pan.

In a large bowl, mix together the flour, sugar, spices, baking soda,
and salt. Make a well in the middle and pour in the beaten eggs and
the honey. Stir only enough to mix thoroughly.

Pour into the prepared springform and sprinkle the top with the
chopped nuts. Bake for 1 hour and 15 minutes, or until the top springs
back when touched. Cool in the pan on a rack. The cake will sink
slightly in the middle as it cools.

# HONEY TAFFY
## (Alvakhazi)

Another traditional New Year's treat.

MAKES ABOUT 2 DOZEN PIECES

**2 cups honey**

In a deep saucepan cook the honey over medium heat for 20 to 25 minutes, until it reaches the soft crack stage (264° F. on a candy thermometer). Allow it to cool until just barely lukewarm, then beat with a wooden spoon until light and creamy, about 5 minutes. Scrape the thickened honey out onto a buttered marble slab or cookie sheet and then, with lightly greased hands, stretch the taffy into a rope. Double one end of the rope back onto the other. Continue pulling and working the taffy until it is stiff and very pale. Cut into 1-inch pieces and wrap in wax paper.

# WHEAT BERRIES
# WITH HONEY
## (Korkoti)

*K*orkoti is cousin to two other wheat berry preparations that are sweetened with sugar: the Turkish *hedik,* with chick-peas and poppy seeds; and the Armenian *hadig,* using pomegranate seeds and raisins. In Georgia, *korkoti* is sometimes made in celebration of a baby's first tooth. Since the wheat berries remain chewy, I very much doubt that one tooth suffices for chewing, but their ultrasweet taste could cause even adults to coo.

SERVES 8

> 1 cup wheat berries
> 2¼ cups water
> Pinch salt
> ¼ cup sugar
> ¼ cup honey
> ½ cup shelled walnuts, ground

Place the wheat berries in a heavy saucepan with the water and salt. Bring to a boil and cook over low heat until all the water has been absorbed, 1½ to 2 hours. The grains will be chewy. Stir in the remaining ingredients while the wheat berries are still warm. Serve warm or at room temperature.

# SWEETENED PUMPKIN WITH WALNUTS
## (Kvakhi Nigvzit)

Here, ground walnuts and sugar sweeten boiled pumpkin for a healthy dessert. Either pumpkin or winter squash may be used in this recipe.

SERVES 6

   1 small (2-pound) pumpkin
   1 cup shelled walnuts
   ⅓ cup sugar

Slice the pumpkin in half and remove the seeds and stringy fibers. Peel and cut the pumpkin into chunks about 1 inch x 2 inches. Boil in salted water until tender, 12 to 15 minutes. Drain well.

   Finely grind the walnuts with the sugar. Place the pumpkin pieces in a bowl and mash to break them up slightly (chunks should still remain). Stir in the walnut-sugar mixture. Serve hot as a porridge or at room temperature for dessert.

# GRAPE JUICE AND CORNMEAL SQUARES
## (Pelamushi)

*Pelamushi* is one of the most interesting and original Georgian foods. Brilliantly purple, cut into diamonds and arranged on a decorative platter, *pelamushi* is deceptive: No one would guess that it is a simple mixture of concentrated grape juice and cornmeal, a grape-flavored polenta. The only similar recipe I have seen is for *panvinesco,* prepared in the wine-growing regions of Italy and calling for vino cotto or cooked wine mixed with semolina.

In my American adaptation of *pelamushi,* I add some sweet, heavy wine to grape juice to approximate the full flavor of the concentrated Georgian *badagi. Pelamushi* must be kept at cool room temperature, since refrigeration destroys its texture.

MAKES ABOUT 3 DOZEN PIECES

1½ cups fine white cornmeal
3 cups unsweetened grape juice
1 cup concord grape wine

In a food processor, finely grind the cornmeal. Pour the grape juice and wine into a 2-quart saucepan and gradually stir in the cornmeal, mixing well. Bring the mixture to a boil and cook over medium heat, stirring from time to time, for 15 minutes. Rinse a 9- x 12-inch metal pan with cold water; pour in the thickened cornmeal mixture, smoothing the top with a knife. Cool at room temperature and cut into 2-inch diamonds.

# MENUS

## A NEW YEAR'S FEAST
✱
*Pickled Cabbage Rose*
*Georgian Cheese Bread or Bean Bread*
*Beef Patties*
*Beet Purée*
*Cabbage with Walnuts*
*Turkey* Satsivi
*Cooked Cheese with Mint*
*Roast Suckling Pig or Chicken with Herbs*
*Candied Walnuts*

## ST. NINO'S DAY CELEBRATION
✱
*Herbed Kidney Beans*
*Chicken Giblets with Walnuts*
*Flattened Chicken with Green Bean* Borani
*Dessert "Peaches"*

## A HEARTY WINTER MEAL
✱
*Braised Lamb Chops or Beef Stew*
*Fresh Mozzarella*
*Corncakes*
*Tea Cake*

## A FAMILY DINNER
✱
*Garlic Fried Chicken*
*Cauliflower with Egg or Stuffed Eggplant*
*Feijoa Relish with Tea*

# AN ELEGANT SUPPER
✳

*Lemony Chicken Soup*
*Salmon Buglama*
*Boiled New Potatoes*
*Walnut Pastry*

# A CASUAL SUPPER
✳

*Hearty Lamb Soup*
*Crusty Peasant Bread*
*Fresh Fruit*

# AN EVENING REFRESHER
✳

*Red Bean Soup or Beef Soup with Herbs*
*Crusty White Bread*
*Red Pepper Pickle*

# A QUIET DINNER WITH FRIENDS
✳

*Veal Stew with Tomatoes and Herbs*
*Boiled Rice*
*Spice Bread or Lemon Tea Cake*

# A MOONLIT SUPPER IN THE ARBOR
✳

*Marinated Grilled Beef or Grilled Meat with Cilantro Sauce*
*Eggplant with Garlic*
*Beets with Cherry Sauce*
*Fresh Herb and Egg Salad*
*Fresh Fruit*

# A HIGHLANDS PICNIC
✳

*Grilled Trout with Tarragon*
*Potato Bread*
*Walnut Roll or Sweet Fruit Leather*

# A FEAST AT SUMMER SOLSTICE
✶

*Salmon in Vinegar Sauce*
*Roast Chicken with Blackberry Sauce or Chicken* Bazhe
*Cheese and Herb Bread*
*Green Bean Purée or Eggplant with Garlic*
*Butter Pastry*

# A WINE COUNTRY REPAST
✶

*Cold Fruit Soup*
*Beef Patties*
*Green Bean Salad*
*Walnut-Raisin Torte*

# A LAVISH LUNCH
✶

*Pickled Garlic or Pickled Leeks*
*Endless Bowls Full of Dumplings*
*Cornelian Cherry Preserves with Tea*

# A HARVEST DINNER
✶

*Eggplant Caviar with Crackerbread*
*Lamb and Vegetable Stew*
*Lady Apple Preserves*

# VEGETARIAN'S DELIGHT
✶

*Herbed Potatoes with Eggs or Baked Noodles with Cheese*
*Kidney Beans with Plum Sauce*
*Vegetable Medley*
*Grape Juice and Cornmeal Squares*

# A GLOSSARY OF GEORGIAN CULINARY TERMS

*Adzhapsandali.* A vegetable medley, like a Georgian ratatouille, which usually contains eggplant, potatoes, onions, green peppers, tomatoes, garlic, and herbs.

*Adzhika.* A favorite condiment made from hot peppers, similar to Mexican salsa.

*Badagi.* Freshly pressed grape juice *(isrimi)* that has been boiled until thick and concentrated.

*Basturma.* Marinated grilled meat.

*Bazhe.* A simple sauce made of pounded walnuts, garlic, and water.

*Borani.* Cooked vegetables such as green beans or spinach, mixed with yogurt and often served with fried chicken.

*Buglama.* A delicate stew of meat or fish with herbs.

*Chacha.* Georgian vodka.

*Chakapuli.* Spicy lamb stew.

*Chakhokhbili.* Braised poultry with onions and tomatoes.

*Chanakhi.* A hearty lamb and vegetable stew cooked slowly in an earthenware pot.

*Chikhirtma.* Chicken (or sometimes lamb) soup enriched with eggs and flavored with saffron.

*Churchkhela.* Georgian national sweet made by stringing nuts and dipping them into thickened grape juice.

*Danduri.* Purslane, eaten both raw and steamed.

*Dzhondzholi.* A garlicky, long-stemmed green usually eaten pickled.

*Gomi.* The name of an ancient milletlike grain, now used to refer to grits.

*Gozinaki.* Traditional New Year's sweet of candied walnuts in honey.

*Isrimi.* Verjuice (freshly pressed grape juice), used in cooking.

*Ketsi.* A red clay dish used for cooking over an open fire.

*Khachapuri.* The ubiquitous cheese bread, made with a variety of doughs ranging from flaky pastry to a yeast-raised crust.

*Kharcho.* Aromatic soup of beef or lamb.

*Khashi.* Tripe soup, said to cure hangovers.

*Khinkali.* Meat- or cheese-filled dumplings, the Georgian wonton or ravioli.

*Khmeli-suneli.* A spice mixture that gives Georgian food its characteristic taste. Most mixtures contain ground dried coriander seed, basil, dill, parsley, fenugreek, summer savory, bay leaf, mint, and dried marigold petals.

*Kvatsarakhi.* Concentrated sour syrup made from barberries.

*Kvevri.* Clay amphora for aging and storing wine.

*Lobio.* The Georgian word for "beans," both fresh green beans and dried kidney beans.

*Machari.* Young wine.

*Marani.* Wine cellar, where *kvevris* are stored. Also refers to a ceremonial vessel with numerous spouts used for pouring wine.

*Masharabi.* Sweetened pomegranate syrup.

*Matsoni.* Yogurt. Georgian yogurt is creamy and tart, made from both cow's milk and water-buffalo milk.

*Mchadi.* Cornmeal cake cooked in a *ketsi* over an open flame or in a cast-iron skillet on the stove. A specialty of western Georgia.

*Mkhali* (also *pkhali*). The generic term for a vegetable purée, traditionally mixed by hand.

*Mtsvadi.* Grilled fresh meat, what we know as shish-kebab.

*Naduyi.* Cheese made from the whey of cow's milk and often served mixed with fresh herbs. *Naduyi* is virtually fat free and is considered a good preventive against sclerosis.

*Puri.* Georgian bread, baked in a clay oven or *toné.*

*Rtveli.* The wine harvest.

*Satsivi.* A famous Georgian spiced walnut sauce, often enriched with egg yolks. It is served over poultry, vegetables, or fish. *Satsivi* is also the name by which the finished dish is known.

*Satsnakheli.* The traditional wooden or stone wine press.

*Suluguni.* A mild cow's milk cheese used as a filling for *khachapuri.*

*Tabaka.* Whole, flattened chicken fried under a heavy weight and served with a variety of sauces.

*Tamada.* The master of ceremonies at a Georgian feast.

*Tkemali.* The sour plum *prunus divaricata* that grows throughout Georgia, as well as the piquant sauce made from it, used as both condiment and seasoning.

*Tklapi.* Dried fruit leather.

*Tolma.* Stuffed vegetables.

*Toné.* The traditional clay oven used for baking bread.

*Tsitsmati.* A peppery salad green not unlike arugula.

# SELECTED
# BIBLIOGRAPHY

Following is an annotated list of some of the more readily available books and articles that I used in researching this cookbook.

## Cuisine

The most thorough survey of Georgian cooking remains Tamara Sulak-velidze's pioneer compilation, *Gruzinskie bliuda* (Georgian Dishes), published in Russian by the Georgian Ministry of Trade (Tbilisi, 1959). A second edition has recently been issued by Sabchota Sakartvelo Publishers (Tbilisi, 1988). A highly abridged edition of the original book was published in this country in Russian by Chalidze Publications (New York, 1982). There also exists an abridged pirate edition published in Israel under the name *Gruzinskaia kukhnia* (Georgian Cuisine), by S. and N. Shtromberg (Tel Aviv, 1986).

A wonderful introduction to Georgian food by Helen and George Papashvily can be found in *Russian Cooking,* part of the Time-Life series called Foods of the World (New York, 1969). George Papashvily grew up in Georgia and, in addition to excellent recipes, he provides a colorful portrait of his homeland.

V. V. Pokhlebkin has an interesting chapter on Georgian food in his *Natsional'nye kukhni nashikh narodov* (The National Cuisines of Our Peoples), published in Moscow in 1978. In addition to offering an assortment of recipes, Pokhlebkin provides a fairly thorough overview of Georgian cuisine.

For a detailed account of the foodways of the inhabitants of Georgia's mountainous regions, see N. P. Dzhikia's *Kul'tura pitaniia gruzinskikh gortsev (The Dietary Culture of the Georgian Highlanders),* published in Tbilisi in 1988. And for a concise introduction to Abkhazian cookery, G. G. Kopeshavidze's *Abkhazskaia kukhnia* (Abkhazian Cuisine), published in Sukhumi in 1989, is useful.

Two interesting articles describe toasting in Georgia, one from a socio-linguistic perspective, the other from an anthropological one. Dee

Ann Holisky's "The Rules of the *Supra* or How to Drink in Georgian," in *Annual of the Society for the Study of Caucasia,* vol. 1, 1989, pages 22–40, is the most comprehensive treatment in English of the etiquette of toasting. See also Gerald Mars and Yochanan Altman, "Alternative mechanism of distribution in a Soviet economy," in *Constructive Drinking: Perspectives on Drink from Anthropology* (Cambridge, 1987), pages 270–279, edited by Mary Douglas.

## Culinary Influences

For further information on external influences on Georgian cuisine, the following books are helpful: Jill Norman's *The Complete Book of Spices* (New York, 1991) provides a history of spices as well as a wonderful array of spice mixtures from all parts of the world. Theodora Fitzgibbon's *The Food of the Western World* (New York, 1976) has a good deal of information on individual spices and herbs. For northern Indian culinary practices, see Madhur Jaffrey, *A Taste of India* (New York, 1986). And for the history of Turkish cuisine, see both *Nevin Halici's Turkish Cookbook* (London, 1989) and Ayla Algar's *Classical Turkish Cooking* (New York, 1991).

## History and Culture

Happily, the best general work on Georgia's history and culture is written in English. W.E.D. Allen's *A History of the Georgian People* (2nd edition, New York, 1971) is the classic in the field, offering in elegant prose a survey of Georgian life "from the beginning down to the Russian conquest in the nineteenth century."

Another useful volume providing an overview of the development of the Georgian nation is *The Georgians* by David Lang (New York, 1966).

For information on early Georgian civilization, an excellent source is Charles Burney and David Marshall Lang's *The Peoples of the Hills: Ancient Ararat and Caucasus* (London, 1971).

A second book that focuses on the early Georgians is Ya. A. Kikvidze's *Zemledelie i zemledel'cheskii kul't v drevnei Gruzii* (Agriculture and the Cult of Agriculture in Ancient Georgia), published in Tbilisi in 1988. Kikvidze gives much valuable information about early Georgian agricultural practices and the development of viticulture.

For the evolution of Georgian foodways, see N. G. Volkova and G. N. Dzhavakhishvili's *Bytovaia kul'tura Gruzii XIX–XX vekov: traditsii i innovatsii* (Daily Culture in Georgia in the 19th and 20th Centuries: Traditions and Innovations), published in Moscow in 1982. This book also contains fascinating chapters on kitchen arrangements and wedding rituals.

A recent contribution to Georgian studies, and one of the few that treats the Soviet period, is Ronald Grigor Suny's *The Making of Modern Georgia* (Bloomington, Indiana, 1988).

Georgi Z. Pitskhelauri, M.D., has written a rather curious volume on Georgian longevity. *The Longliving of Soviet Georgia,* translated and edited by Gari Lesnoff-Caravaglia (New York, 1982), contains some information about the benefits of the Georgian diet.

## Art

A beautiful, and complete, edition of Pirosmani's paintings, *Niko Pirosmani,* has been published in English by Aurora Art Publishers (Leningrad, 1983). This volume also includes charming sepia photographs of old Tbilisi and its inhabitants.

For a history and illustrations of Georgia's traditional arts, see Rusudan Mepisashvili and Vakhtang Tsintsadze's *The Arts of Ancient Georgia* (London, 1979).

## Language and Literature

The standard American textbook for Georgian is Howard I. Aronson, *Georgian: A Reading Grammar* (Columbus, Ohio, 1982).

Shota Rustaveli's epic poem has been issued by Sabchota Sakartvelo Publishers in a lovely English translation by Venera Urushadze. See *The Knight in the Panther's Skin* (Tbilisi, 1986).

## Travel

My favorite account of travels to Georgia is *The Travels of Sir John Chardin into Persia and the East-Indies Through the Black Sea and the Country of Colchis* (London, 1686). Chardin has a good eye for detail and delights in recounting the cultural oddities he finds. His narrative contains a good deal of information about seventeenth-century Georgian eating habits.

Similarly engaging are the tales told by the Turkish traveler Evliyá Efendí, *Narrative of Travels in Europe, Asia, and Africa in the Seventeenth Century,* translated by The Ritter Joseph von Hammer (London, 1834).

Even earlier than Chardin and Efendí, Marco Polo and Friar William of Rubruck traveled through Georgia and mentioned it in their notes. For entertaining reading, see *The Travels of Marco Polo,* translated by Sir Henry Yule (London, 1921), and *The Mission of Friar William of Rubruck,* translated by Peter Jackson (London, 1990).

Alexandre Dumas left an extremely appealing memoir of his travels to the Caucasus, *Le Caucase; depuis Prométhée jusqu'à Chamyll* (Paris, 1859).

This book is available in English translation as *Adventures in Caucasia*, translated and edited by A. E. Murch (Westport, Connecticut, 1975).

The charming descriptions of Georgia by the Vicomte Eugène Melchior de Vogüé, "Through the Caucasus," are in the June 1890 issue of *Harper's Monthly*.

As a woman, Odette Keun saw Georgia from quite a different perspective than the more frequent male travelers to the region. Her book, *In the Land of the Golden Fleece: Through Independent Menshevist Georgia* (London, 1924), contains many perceptive passages.

A more recent visitor to the Caucasus, the British diplomat Sir Fitzroy Maclean, has written a lively book that includes historical fact and legend in equal measure. His *To Caucasus: The End of All the Earth* (Boston, 1976) has the advantage of lovely color photographs that give the reader a good sense of Georgian landscape and life.

For those planning a trip to Georgia, Planeta Publishers in Moscow offer a useful English-language handbook, *Tbilisi: A Guide* (Moscow, 1988), which covers not only the city of Tbilisi but most of the Georgian republic.

# INDEX

RU

CAUCAS

Mestia ■

ABKHAZIA

SVANETI

RACHA

SAMEGRELO

■ Khobi     ■ Kutaisi

Rioni R.

BLACK
SEA

GEOR

IMERETI

GURIA

LIKHI

■ Poti

ADZHARIA

■ Batumi

T U R K E Y

0 ⊢——————⊣ 50 miles

0 ⊢——————⊣ 50 kilometers